Granger Index

RECITATIONS

❧ ❧ FOR ❧ ❧

YOUNGER CHILDREN

RECITATIONS
FOR
YOUNGER CHILDREN

COMPILED AND EDITED
BY
GRACE GAIGE

Granger Poetry Library

GRANGER BOOK CO., INC.
GREAT NECK, N.Y.

FIRST PUBLISHED 1927
REPRINTED 1979

INTERNATIONAL STANDARD BOOK NUMBER
0-89609-134-1

LIBRARY OF CONGRESS CATALOG NUMBER
78-74816

PRINTED IN THE UNITED STATES OF AMERICA

TO

E. H.

ACKNOWLEDGMENTS

For permission to use copyrighted material included in this volume, the editor is indebted to the following authors and publishers, whose courtesy is hereby gratefully acknowledged:

The Bobbs-Merrill Company, the poems by James Whitcomb Riley and William Herschell.

Albert & Charles Boni, the poems by Nathalia Crane.

The Century Co., the poems by Malcolm Douglas, Pauline Frances Camp and Rose Mill Powers.

Dodge Publishing Company, the poem by Edmund Vance Cooke.

George H. Doran Company, the poems by Lizette Woodworth Reese, Amelia J. Burr and Rose Fyleman.

E. P. Dutton & Company, the poems by James W. Foley and Eleanor Farjeon.

Harcourt, Brace and Company, the poems by Carl Sandburg and Louis Untermeyer.

Henry Holt and Company, the poems by Walter de la Mare and Robert Frost.

Houghton Mifflin Company, the poems by Frank Dempster Sherman, Amy Lowell, James Russell Lowell, Thomas Bailey Aldrich, Abbie Farwell Brown and Ralph Waldo Emerson.

George W. Jacobs & Company, the poem by Rupert Sargent Holland.

P. J. Kenedy & Sons, the poem by Father Ryan.

Alfred A. Knopf, the poems by W. H. Davies.

Little, Brown and Company, the poem by Helen Hunt Jackson.

Lothrop, Lee & Shepard Co., the poem by Emilie Poulsson.

The Macmillan Company, the poems by Sara Teasdale, John Masefield and James Stephens.

Minton, Balch & Company, the poems by Dorothy Aldis.

Thomas Bird Mosher, the poem by Lizette Woodworth Reese.

L. C. Page Company, the poems by Laura E. Richards.

The Penn Publishing Company, the poems by A. L. Mitchell, Lizzie M. Hadley and Esther W. Buxton.

The Reilly & Lee Co., the poem by Edgar A. Guest.

Charles Scribner's Sons, the poems by Oliver Herford, Henry van Dyke, Mary Mapes Dodge, Eugene Field, Robert Louis Stevenson and Henry R. Stoddard.

Frederick A. Stokes Company, the poems by Eleanor Farjeon, Hilda Conkling and Annette Wynne.

The Viking Press, the poems by Elizabeth Madox Roberts.

Frederick Warne & Co., Ltd., the poems by Edward Lear and Kate Greenaway.

Albert Whitman & Co., the poems by Clara J. Denton.

Yale University Press, the poem by John Farrar.

The editor is deeply grateful to the following poets, editors, magazines and individual holders of copyright for permission graciously given her to use the following poems:

Ruth Collat, for permission to use "Speckles."

Hamlin Garland, for permission to use "Do you Fear the Wind?".

Charles S. Kinnison, for permission to use "When Mother's Sick."

Richard Le Gallienne, for permission to use "A Child's Evensong."

Edwin Markham, for permission to use "The League of Love in Action."

The Estate of E. Nesbit, for permission to use "Child Song in Spring" and "Baby Seed Song."

Lizette Woodworth Reese, for permission to use "A Christmas Folksong."

Lilly Robinson, for permission to use "I'd Rather Be Me" and "My Mouse."

S. Virginia Sherwood, for permission to use "Dreams."

Eileen Wickizer, for permission to use "The North Wind."

CONTENTS

NURSERY LAND

PRAYERS

HUMOR

SONGS OF JOY

PATRIOTIC

DAYS WE CELEBRATE

NURSERY LAND

THE QUEEN OF HEARTS

THE Queen of Hearts
   She made some tarts,
All on a summer's day;
   The Knave of Hearts
   He stole those tarts,
And took them clean away.

The King of Hearts
   Called for the tarts,
And beat the Knave full sore;
   The Knave of Hearts
   Brought back the tarts,
And vowed he'd steal no more.

UNKNOWN

MY BED IS A BOAT

MY bed is like a little boat;
   Nurse helps me in when I embark;
She girds me in my sailor's coat,
   And starts me in the dark.

At night, I go on board and say
   Good night to all my friends on shore;
I shut my eyes and sail away
   And see and hear no more.

And sometimes things to bed I take,
   As prudent sailors have to do;
Perhaps a slice of wedding cake,
   Perhaps a toy or two.

All night across the dark we steer;
   But when the day returns at last,
Safe in my room, beside the pier,
   I find my vessel fast.

R. L. STEVENSON

3

BABY LAND

"HOW many miles to Baby Land?"
  "Any one can tell;
    Up one flight,
    To the right;
  Please to ring the bell."

"What can you see in Baby Land?"
  "Little folks in white—
    Downy heads,
    Cradle beds
  Faces pure and bright!"

"What do they do in Baby Land?"
  "Dream and wake and play,
    Laugh and crow,
    Shout and grow;
  Jolly times have they!"

"Who is the Queen of Baby Land?"
"Mother, kind and sweet;
    And her love,
    Born above,
  Guides the little feet."

GEORGE COOPER

STRANGE LANDS

WHERE do you come from, Mr. Jay?
  "From the land of Play, from the land of Play."
And where can that be, Mr. Jay?
  "Far away—far away."

Where do you come from, Mrs. Dove?
"From the land of Love, from the land of Love."
And how do you get there, Mrs. Dove?
  "Look above—look above."

Where do you come from, Baby Miss?
"From the land of Bliss, from the land of Bliss."
And what is the way there, Baby Miss?
"Mother's kiss—mother's kiss."

LAURENCE ALMA-TADEMA

"THERE WAS A LITTLE GIRL"

THERE was a little girl, who had a little curl
Right in the middle of her forehead,
And when she was good, she was very, very good,
But when she was bad she was horrid.

She stood on her head, on her little trundle-bed,
With nobody by for to hinder;
She screamed and she squalled, she yelled and she bawled,
And drummed her little heels against the winder.

Her mother heard the noise, and thought it was the boys
Playing in the empty attic,
She rushed upstairs, and caught her unawares,
And spanked her, most emphatic.

HENRY WADSWORTH LONGFELLOW

PETER PIPER

PETER PIPER picked a peck of pickled peppers;
A peck of pickled peppers Peter Piper picked;
If Peter Piper picked a peck of pickled peppers,
Where's the peck of pickled peppers Peter Piper picked?

UNKNOWN

OLD KING COLE

OLD King Cole
Was a merry old soul,
And a merry old soul was he;
He called for his pipe,

And he called for his bowl,
And he called for his fiddlers three.
Every fiddler, he had a fiddle,
And a very fine fiddle had he;
Twee tweedle dee, tweedle dee,
Went the fiddlers.
Oh, there's none so rare,
As can compare
With King Cole and his fiddlers three!

UNKNOWN

CRADLE SONG

HUSHABY, baby, on the tree top,
When the wind blows the cradle will rock;
When the bough breaks the cradle will fall,
Down will come baby and cradle and all.

UNKNOWN

LITTLE BOPEEP

LITTLE BOPEEP has lost her sheep,
And can't tell where to find them;
Leave them alone, and they'll come home,
And bring their tails behind them.

Little Bopeep fell fast asleep,
And dreamed she heard them bleating;
But when she awoke, she found it a joke,
For they were still a-fleeting.

Then up she took her little crook,
Determined for to find them;
She found them indeed, but it made her heart bleed,
For they'd left their tails behind them.

UNKNOWN

THE BEST NONSENSE RIME

THERE was once a young lady of Riga
    Who went for a ride on a tiger:
They returned from the ride
With the lady inside
And a smile on the face of the tiger.

COSMO MONKHOUSE

A NURSERY SONG

OH, Peterkin Pout and Gregory Grout
    Are two little goblins black.
Full oft from my house I've driven them out,
    But somehow they come back.

They clamber up to the baby's mouth,
    And pull the corners down;
They perch aloft on the baby's brow,
    And twist it into frown.

And one says "Must!" and t'other says "Can't!"
And one says "Shall!" and t'other says "Sha'n't!"
Oh, Peterkin Pout and Gregory Grout,
I pray you now, from my house keep out!

But Samuel Smile and Lemuel Laugh
    Are two little fairies light;
They're always ready for fun and chaff,
    And sunshine is their delight.

And when they creep into Baby's eyes,
    Why, there the sunbeams are;
And when they peep through her rosy lips,
    Her laughter rings near and far.

And one says "Please!" and t'other says "Do!"
And both together say "I love you!"
So, Lemuel Laugh and Samuel Smile,
Come in, my dears, and tarry awhile!

LAURA E. RICHARDS

I'LL TRY

TWO Robin Redbreasts built their nest
    Within a hollow tree;
The hen sat quietly at home,
The cock sang merrily;
And all the little robins said:
"Wee, wee, wee, wee, wee, wee."

One day the sun was warm and bright,
And shining in the sky.
Cock Robin said: "My little dears,
'Tis time you learned to fly";
And all the little young ones said:
"I'll try, I'll try, I'll try."

I know a child, and who she is
I'll tell you by and by.
When mother says "Do this," or "that,"
She says "What for?" and "Why?"
She'd be a better child by far
If she would say "I'll try."

UNKNOWN

LONDON BRIDGE

LONDON bridge is broken down
    Dance o'er my Lady Lee;
London bridge is broken down,
    With a gay lady.

How shall we build it up again?
    Dance o'er my Lady Lee;
How shall we build it up again?
    With a gay lady.

Silver and gold will be stole away,
    Dance o'er my Lady Lee;
Silver and gold will be stole away,
    With a gay lady.

Build it up again with iron and steel,
   Dance o'er my Lady Lee;
Build it up with iron and steel,
   With a gay lady.

Iron and steel will bend and bow,
   Dance o'er my Lady Lee;
Iron and steel will bend and bow,
   With a gay lady.

Build it up with wood and clay,
   Dance o'er my Lady Lee;
Build it up with wood and clay,
   With a gay lady.

Wood and clay will wash away,
   Dance o'er my Lady Lee;
Wood and clay will wash away,
   With a gay lady.

Build it up with stone so strong,
   Dance o'er my Lady Lee;
Huzza 'twill last for ages long,
   With a gay lady.

UNKNOWN

A FARMER WENT TROTTING

A FARMER went trotting upon his gray mare;
   Bumpety, bumpety, bump!
With his daughter behind him, so rosy and fair;
Lumpety, lumpety, lump!

A raven cried croak! and they all tumbled down;
Bumpety, bumpety, bump!
The mare broke her knees, and the farmer his crown;
Lumpety, lumpety, lump!

The mischievous raven flew laughing away;
Bumpety, bumpety, bump!
And vowed he would serve them the same the next day;
Lumpety, lumpety, lump!

UNKNOWN

LITTLE FRED

WHEN little Fred
        Was called to bed,
He always acted right;
    He kissed Mamma,
    And then Papa,
And wished them all good night.

    He made no noise,
    Like naughty boys,
But gently up the stairs
    Directly went,
    When he was sent,
And always said his prayers.

UNKNOWN

THE SIESTA

SAND MAN, Sand Man, why do you come so soon?
    You shouldn't come till six o'clock, and here you are at
        noon!
I've swept the floor and dressed my doll, and made a pie or
        two.
But this is Monday, and I have my washing yet to do.
I wish you'd wait until I get my clothes out on the line,
Before you throw your slumber-dust in Dolly's eyes and
        mine.
Sand Man, Sand Man, please to go away;
I'll welcome you at six to-night, but not at noon to-day!

CARL WERNER

THE BREAKFAST SONG

A T five o'clock he milks the cow,
   The busy farmer's man.
At six o'clock he strains the milk
   And pours it in the can.

At seven o'clock the milkman's horse
   Must go to town—"get up!"
At eight o'clock Nurse Karen pours
   The milk in Baby's cup.

At five o'clock the Baby sleeps
   As sound as sound can be.
At six o'clock he laughs and shouts,
   So wide awake is he.

At seven o'clock he's in his bath,
   At eight o'clock he's dressed,
Just when the milk is ready, too,
   So you can guess the rest.

EMILIE POULSSON

WHAT ARE LITTLE BOYS MADE OF

W HAT are little boys made of, made of,
   What are little boys made of?
Snaps and snails, and puppy dogs' tails;
And that's what little boys are made of, made of.

What are little girls made of, made of,
What are little girls made of?
Sugar and spice, and all that's nice;
And that's what little girls are made of, made of.

UNKNOWN

FAIRYLAND

FAIRIES *

THERE are fairies at the bottom of our garden!
  It's not so very, very far away;
You pass the gardener's shed and you just keep straight
    ahead—
I do so hope they've really come to stay.
There's a little wood, with moss in it and beetles,
And a little stream that quietly runs through;
You wouldn't think they'd dare to come merrymaking
    there—
        Well, they do.

There are fairies at the bottom of our garden!
They often have a dance on summer nights;
The butterflies and bees make a lovely little breeze.
And the rabbits stand about and hold the lights.
Did you know that they could sit upon the moonbeams
And pick a little star to make a fan,
And dance away up there in the middle of the air?
        Well, they can.

There are fairies at the bottom of our garden!
You cannot think how beautiful they are;
They all stand up and sing when the Fairy Queen and King
Come gently floating down upon their car.
The King is very proud and *very* handsome;
The Queen—now can you guess who that could be
(She's a little girl all day, but at night she steals away)?
        Well—it's ME!

                                    ROSE FYLEMAN

---

* From *Fairies and Chimneys* by Rose Fyleman; copyright, 1920,
George H. Doran Company, Publishers.
15

QUEEN MAB

A LITTLE fairy comes at night;
  Her eyes are blue, her hair is brown,
With silver spots upon her wings,
  And from the moon she flutters down.

She has a little silver wand,
  And when a good child goes to bed,
She waves her wand from right to left,
  And makes a circle round its head.

And then it dreams of pleasant things—
  Fountains filled with fairy fish,
And trees that bear delicious fruit,
  And bow their branches at a wish;

Of arbors filled with dainty scents
  From lovely flowers that never fade,
Bright flies that glitter in the sun,
  And glowworms shining in the shade;

And talking birds with gifted tongues
  For singing songs and telling tales,
And pretty dwarfs to show the way
  Through fairy hills and fairy dales.

THOMAS HOOD

THE FAIRY BOOK

IN summer, when the grass is thick, if mother has the
    time,
She shows me with her pencil how a poet makes a rhyme,
And often she is sweet enough to choose a leafy nook,
Where I cuddle up so closely when she reads the Fairy
  Book.

In winter when the corn's asleep, and birds are not in song,
And crocuses and violets have been away too long,
Dear mother puts her thimble by in answer to my look,
And I cuddle up so closely when she reads the Fairy Book.

And mother tells the servants that of course they must con-
    trive
To manage all the household things from four till half-
    past five,
For we really cannot suffer interruption from the cook,
When we cuddle close together with the happy Fairy Book.

NORMAN GALE

THE LIGHT-HEARTED FAIRY

OH, who is so merry, so merry, heigh ho!
    As the lighted-hearted fairy? heigh ho,
        Heigh ho!
    He dances and sings
    To the sound of his wings
With a hey and a heigh and a ho!

Oh, who is so merry, so airy, heigh ho!
As the light-headed fairy? heigh ho,
        Heigh ho!
    His nectar he sips
    From the primroses' lips
With a hey and a heigh and a ho!

Oh, who is so merry, so merry, heigh ho!
As the light-footed fairy? heigh ho!
        Heigh ho!
    The night is his noon
    And his sun is the moon,
With a hey and a heigh and a ho!

UNKNOWN

VERY NEARLY

I NEVER *quite* saw fairy folk
    A-dancing in the glade,
Where, just beyond the hollow oak,
    Their broad green rings are laid:
But, while behind that oak I hid,
One day I very nearly did!

I never *quite* saw mermaids rise
  Above the twilight sea,
When sands, left wet, 'neath sunset skies,
  Are blushing rosily:
But—all alone, those rocks amid—
One day I very nearly did!

I never *quite* saw Goblin Grim,
  Who haunts our lumber room
And pops his head above the rim
  Of that oak chest's deep gloom:
But once—when mother raised the lid—
I very, very nearly did!

QUEENIE SCOTT-HOPPER

THE FAIRY BOOK

WHEN Mother takes the Fairy Book
    And we curl up to hear,
'Tis "All aboard for Fairyland!"
  Which seems to be so near.

For soon we reach the pleasant place
  Of Once Upon a Time,
Where birdies sing the hour of day,
  And flowers talk in rhyme;

Where Bobby is a velvet Prince,
  And where I am a Queen;
Where one can talk with animals,
  And walk about unseen;

Where Little People live in nuts,
  And ride on butterflies,
And wonders kindly come to pass
  Before your very eyes;

Where candy grows on every bush,
    And playthings on the trees,
And visitors pick basketfuls
    As often as they please.

It is the nicest time of day—
    Though Bedtime is so near—
When Mother takes the Fairy Book
    And we curl up to hear.

ABBIE FARWELL BROWN

THE RAINBOW FAIRIES

TWO little clouds one summer's day
    Went flying through the sky.
They went so fast they bumped their heads,
    And both began to cry.

Old Father Sun looked out and said,
    "Oh, never mind, my dears,
I'll send my little fairy folk
    To dry your falling tears."

One fairy came in violet,
    And one in indigo,
In blue, green, yellow, orange, red—
    They made a pretty row.

They wiped the cloud tears all away,
    And then from out the sky,
Upon a line the sunbeams made,
    They hung their gowns to dry.

LIZZIE M. HADLEY

THE SATURDAYS' PARTY IN FAIRYLAND

ALL the Saturdays met one day
    (Each was very polite, they say),
They shook each other by the hand,
And had a party in Fairyland!

They wouldn't let any Monday in,
And not one Tuesday at all could win
Her way past the supercilious crowd!
And Wednesdays—why, they weren't allowed!

Thursdays could only stand in the street
And look through the door at the things to eat!
And the Fridays and Sundays pretended they
Didn't like parties, anyway!

But the Saturdays had the greatest fun!
They played "Hopscotch" and "Run sheep run,"
And "Frog in the meadow," and "Pull away!"
And everything else they wanted to play!

They used the Throne for "Musical Chairs"
As if the Fairy Queen's house were theirs!
In rooms enchanted they ran and hid,
And whatever they wished they could do, they did!

And after they'd played and played and played,
They had pink straws in their lemonade!
And the cookies and tarts were like a dream!
And all the Saturdays had ice cream!

I'd my doubts when I heard—and you have yours—
But strange things happen on Foreign Shores!
And they say that the best *fête* ever planned
Was the Saturdays' party in Fairyland!

M. C. DAVIES

PLEASE *

PLEASE be careful where you tread,
   The fairies are about;
Last night, when I had gone to bed,
   I heard them creeping out.

* From *The Fairy Green* by Rose Fyleman; copyright, 1923,
George H. Doran Company, Publishers.

And wouldn't it be a dreadful thing
  To do a fairy harm?
To crush a little delicate wing
  Or bruise a tiny arm?
They're all about the place, I know,
So do be careful where you go.

Please be careful what you say,
  They're often very near,
And though they turn their heads away
  They cannot help but hear.
And think how terribly you would mind
  If, even for a joke,
You said a thing that seemed unkind
  To the dear little fairy folk.
I'm sure they're simply everywhere,
So *promise* me that you'll take care.

ROSE FYLEMAN

PRAYERS

BED CHARM

MATTHEW, Mark, Luke, John,
   Bless the bed that I lie on!
Four corners to my bed,
Four angels round my head,
One at head and one at feet
And two to keep my soul asleep!

UNKNOWN

A CHILD'S PRAYER

GOD make my life a little light,
   Within the world to glow—
A tiny flame that burneth bright,
   Wherever I may go.

God make my life a little flower,
   That bringeth joy to all,
Content to bloom in native bower,
   Although its place be small.

God make my life a little song,
   That comforteth the sad,
That helpeth others to be strong,
   And makes the singer glad.

M. BETHAM EDWARDS

A PRAYER

FATHER, we thank Thee for the night
   And for the pleasant morning light,
For rest and food and loving care,
And all that makes the world so fair.
Help us to do the thing we should,
To be to others kind and good,
In all we do, in all we say,
To grow more loving every day.

UNKNOWN

GOOD NIGHT PRAYER FOR A LITTLE CHILD

FATHER, unto Thee I pray,
    Thou hast guarded me all day;
Safe I am while in Thy sight,
Safely let me sleep to-night.

Bless my friends, the whole world bless,
Help me to learn helpfulness;
Keep me ever in Thy sight:
So to all I say Good Night.

HENRY JOHNSTONE

A CHILD'S MORNING PRAYER

I THANK Thee, Lord, for quiet rest,
    And for Thy care of me:
Oh! let me through this day be blest,
    And kept from harm by Thee.

Oh, let me love Thee! kind Thou art
    To children such as I;
Give me a gentle, holy heart,
    Be Thou my Friend on high.

Help me to please my parents dear,
    And do whate'er they tell;
Bless all my friends, both far and near,
    And keep them safe and well.

MARY LUNDIE DUNCAN

PRAYERS

WHEN I kneel down my prayers to say,
    I must not think of toys or play;
No! I must think what I should be;
To please God who is good to me.

He loves to see a little child
Obedient—patient, too—and mild;
Nor often angry, but inclined
Always to do what's good and kind.

And I must love my dear mamma,
And I must love my dear papa;
And try to please them, and to do
Things that are right, and say what's true.

For God is always pleased to see
Even little children such as we,
Whose hearts (as angels' are above)
Are full of peace and full of love.

FLORA HASTINGS

A CHILD'S WISH

BEFORE AN ALTAR

I WISH I were the little key
That locks Love's Captive in,
And lets Him out to go and free
A sinful heart from sin.

I wish I were the little bell
That tinkles for the Host,
When God comes down each day to dwell
With hearts He loves the most.

I wish I were the chalice fair,
That holds the Blood of Love,
When every flash lights holy prayer
Upon its way above.

I wish I were the little flower
So near the Host's sweet face,
Or like the light that half an hour
Burns on the shrine of grace.

I wish I were the altar where,
  As on His Mother's breast,
Christ nestles, like a child, fore'er
  In Eucharistic rest.

But, oh! my God, I wish the most
  That my poor heart may be
A home all holy for each Host
  That comes in love to me.

ABRAM J. RYAN

HUMOR

THE LITTLE PEACH

A LITTLE peach in the orchard grew—
A little peach of emerald hue;
Warmed by the sun and wet by the dew,
    It grew.

One day, passing the orchard through,
That little peach dawned on the view
Of Johnnie Jones and his Sister Sue—
    Them two.

Up at the peach a club they threw—
Down from the stem on which it grew
Fell that peach of emerald hue—
    Mon Dieu!

John took a bite and Sue a chew,
And then the trouble began to brew—
Trouble the doctor couldn't subdue—
    Too true!

Under the turf where the daisies grew
They planted John and his Sister Sue,
And their little souls to the angels flew—
    Boohoo!

What of that peach of emerald hue,
Warmed by the sun and wet by the dew?
Ah, well, its mission on earth is through—
    Adieu!

EUGENE FIELD

A LITTLE BOY'S TROUBLES

I THOUGHT when I'd learned my letters
    That all of my troubles were done;
But I find myself much mistaken—
    They only have just begun.
Learning to read was awful,
    But nothing like learning to write;
I'd be sorry to have you tell it,
    But my copybook is a sight!

The ink gets over my fingers;
    The pen cuts all sorts of shines,
And won't do at all as I bid it;
    The letters won't stay on the lines,
But go up and down and all over,
    As though they were dancing a jig—
They are there in all shapes and sizes,
    Medium, little, and big.

The tails of the *g's* are so contrary,
    The handles get on the wrong side
Of the *d's*, and the *k's*, and the *h's*,
    Though I've certainly tried and tried
To make them just right; it is dreadful,
    I really don't know what to do,
I'm getting almost distracted—
    My teacher says she is too.

There'd be some comfort in learning
    If one could get through: instead
Of that there are books awaiting
    Quite enough to craze my head.
There's the multiplication table,
    And grammar, and—oh! dear me,
There's no good place for stopping
    When one has begun, I see.

My teacher says, little by little
    To the mountain tops we climb;

It isn't all done in a minute,
   But only a step at a time;
She says that all the scholars,
   All the wise and learned men,
Had each to begin as I do;
   If that's so, where's my pen?

CARLOTTA PERRY

THE LOST CHILD

"I'M losted! Could you find me, please?"
   Poor little frightened baby!
The wind had tossed her golden fleece,
The stones had scratched her dimpled knees,
I stooped and lifted her with ease,
   And softly whispered, "Maybe."

"Tell me your name, my little maid,
   I can't find you without it."
"My name is Shiny-Eyes," she said.
"Yes, but your last?" She shook her head:
"Up to you house 'ey never said
   A single fing about it."

"But dear," I said, "what is your name?"
   "Why, didn't you hear me tell you?
Dest Shiny-Eyes." A bright thought came:
"Yes, when you're good; but when they blame
You, little one—is't just the same
   When mamma has to scold you?"

"My mamma never scolds," she moans,
   A little blush ensuing,
" 'Cept when I've been a-frowing stones,
And then she says," the culprit owns,
"Mehitable Sapphira Jones,
   What has you been a-doing?"

UNKNOWN

PLANTING HIMSELF TO GROW

DEAR little, bright-eyed Willie,
   Always so full of glee,
Always so very mischievous,
   The pride of our home is he.

One bright summer day we found him
   Close by the garden wall,
Standing so grave and dignified
   Beside a sunflower tall.

His tiny feet he had covered
   With the moist and cooling sand;
The stalk of the great, tall sunflower
   He grasped with his chubby hand.

When he saw us standing near him,
   Gazing so wonderingly
At his babyship, he greeted us
   With a merry shout of glee.

We asked our darling what pleased him;
   He replied, with a face aglow,
"Mamma, I'm going to be a man;
   I've planted myself to grow."

UNKNOWN

A JINGLE

WOULDN'T it be funny—
   Wouldn't it, now—
If the dog said "Moo-oo"
   And the cow said "Bow-wow"?
If the cat sang and whistled,
   And the bird said "Mia-ow"?
Wouldn't it be funny—
   Wouldn't it now?

UNKNOWN

A DISPUTE

TOM and Joe quarreled,
    I've heard people tell;
About a queer animal
    Hid in a shell.
"I tell you it walks, sir!"
    Said Tommy to Joe;
"It swims!" cried Joe, loudly,
    "I've seen and I know!"
"It walks!"—"No, it swims!"—
    And the boys grew quite wroth,
But the turtle peeped out,
    Saying, "I can do both!"

A. L. MITCHILL

THAT'S BABY

ONE little row of ten little toes,
    To go along with brand new nose,
Eight little fingers and two new thumbs,
That are just as good as sugar plums—
    That's baby.

One little pair of round, new eyes,
Like a little owl's, so big and wise,
One little place they call a mouth,
Without one tooth from north to south—
    That's baby.

Two little cheeks to kiss all day,
Two little hands so in his way,
A brand new head, not very big,
That seems to need a brand new wig—
    That's baby.

Dear little row of ten little toes!
How much we love them nobody knows;
Ten little kisses on mouth and chin,
What a shame he wasn't born a twin—
    That's baby.

UNKNOWN

A LESSON FOR MAMMA

DEAR mother, if you just could be
    A tiny little girl like me,
And I your mother, you would see
    How nice I'd be to you.
I'd always let you have your way;
I'd never frown at you and say,
    "You are behaving ill to-day;
    Such conduct will not do."

I'd always give you jelly cake
For breakfast, and I'd never shake
My head and say, "You must not take
    So very large a slice."
I'd never say, "My dear, I trust
You will not make me say you *must*
Eat up your oatmeal"; or "The crust,
    You'll find, is very nice."

I'd buy you candy every day;
I'd go down town with you, and say,
"What would my darling like? You may
    Have anything you see."
I'd never say, "My pet, you know
'Tis bad for health and teeth, and so
I cannot let you have it. No;
    It would be wrong in me."

And every day I'd let you wear
Your nicest dress, and never care
If it should get a great big tear;
    I'd only say to you,

"My precious treasure, never mind,
For little clothes *will* tear, I find."
Now, mother, wouldn't that be kind?
   That's just what *I* should do.

I'd never say, "Well, just a *few!*"
I'd let you stop your lessons too;
I'd say, "They are too hard for you,
   Poor child, to understand."
I'd put the books and slates away;
You shouldn't do a thing but play,
And have a party every day;
   Ah-h-h! wouldn't that be grand!

But, mother dear, you cannot grow
Into a little girl, you know,
And I can't be your mother; so
   The only thing to do,
Is just for you to try and see
How very, very nice 'twould be
For *you* to do all this for *me*,
   Now, mother, *couldn't* you?

SYDNEY DAYRE

GROWN UP *

I 'M growing up my mother says—
   To-day she said I'd grown;
The reason why is this: now I
Can do things all alone.

And though I'm glad that I don't need
Some one to brush my hair
And wash my hands and face and button
Buttons everywhere.

---

* From *Everything and Anything* by Dorothy Aldis, courtesy of
Minton, Balch and Company, Publishers.

Although I'm very glad indeed
To help myself instead,
I hope that I won't have to try
TO TUCK MYSELF IN BED.

DOROTHY ALDIS

LOVE

NOW Marjory is Seven Years,
  And I am nine and more.
We went a-strolling after cream
Into a Flatbush Store.

The handsome clerk said, "Ladies, yes,
I'll serve you with a rush."
He looked so very scrumptious that
We both began to blush.

He smiled at us, we smiled at him.
And then he went away;
We were so captivated, yes,
That we forgot to pay.

Of course we could have sauntered back,
And settled, don't you see,
But oh, we could not stain romance
With monetary fee.

NATHALIA CRANE

MOUTHS *

I WISH I had two little mouths
  Like my two hands and feet—
A little mouth to talk with
And one that just could eat.
Because it seems to me mouths have

---

* From *Everything and Anything* by Dorothy Aldis, courtesy of
Minton, Balch and Company, Publishers.

So many things to do—
All the time they want to talk
They are supposed to chew.

DOROTHY ALDIS

GRANDMA'S MISTAKE

POOR Grandma, I do hate to tell her,
    And yet it does seem queer,
She's lived so much longer than I have,
    And I, why, I've known it a year.

Even Alice begins to look doubtful,
    And she is so babyish, too;
And Mamma just laughs at the nonsense,
    But Grandma believes it is true.

I did it all up in brown paper,
    And laid it just there by her plate,
And she put on her glasses so slowly,
    I thought that I never could wait.

And when she had opened the bundle,
    "My gracious!" she said, "how complete!
A dear little box for my knitting;
    Now isn't old Santa Claus sweet?"

UNKNOWN

A CANDY PULL

TWO little maids had a candy pull,
    Once, on a winter's day;
"The very best time that ever was,
    And the sweetest, too!" laughed May.

But mamma frowned, with her comb in hand:
    "There is candy everywhere;
And as if 'tweren't scattered quite enough,
    Here is some in Gracie's hair!"

And Gracie's eyes with tears were blind,
    As she clung to mamma's knee;
"I fink that this is the very worst kind
    Of a candy pull!" sobbed she.

UNKNOWN

THE PRICE HE PAID

TEDDY came to tell his playmate
    Of a most successful trade.
"I've got just the best knife this time—
    Corkscrew, big and little blade,
Real pearl handle—cost a dollar
    At the store a week ago;
But," and here he winked at Tommy,
    "Didn't cost me that, you know.

"No, sir; what I traded for it
    Wasn't worth a dime, I guess.
You have seen the chain Bob gave me—
    Brass all through and nothing less.
Well, he took a fancy to it,
    When I hinted it was gold,
And he swapped his jackknife for it.
    My, but didn't he get sold?"

"Yes, perhaps," was Tommy's answer,
    In a grave and thoughtful way;
"But I think the knife has cost you
    More than I would like to pay."
"You don't think that I got cheated?"
    "Yes," was Tommy's quick reply,
"You could not afford to do it,
    For you had to tell a lie."

UNKNOWN

THE OWNER AWAY

HARK, hark! What's that noise?
Something's the matter with the toys.
Scrub, scrub! Swish, swash!
The biggest doll is trying to wash.

The other dolls are making cake;
The new cookstove is beginning to bake;
The table is setting itself, you see;
They must be expecting friends to tea.

UNKNOWN

AROUND THE WORLD

IN gocart so tiny
My sister I drew;
And I've promised to draw her
The wide world through.

We have not yet started—
I own it with sorrow—
Because our trip's always
Put off till to-morrow.

KATE GREENAWAY

A NEW KIND OF DOLL

"I'M tired of leather dolls," said Belle,
"The sawdust all runs out,
I want one just like baby Nell,"
And Belle began to pout.

"Her eyes shut every night, you see,"
And then she sobbed in grief,
"Mamma, you never buy for me
A doll that's made of beef."

ANNA L. JACK

THE LOST PENNY

IN little Daisy's dimpled hand
   Two bright, new pennies shone;
One was for Rob (at school just then),
The other Daisy's own.
While waiting Rob's return she rolled
Both treasures round the floor,
When suddenly they disappeared,
And one was seen no more.
"Poor Daisy. Is your penny lost?"
Was asked in accents kind.
"Why, no, *mine's* here!" she quickly said,
It's Rob's I cannot find."

UNKNOWN

BABY'S LOGIC

SHE was ironing her dolly's new gown
   Maid Marian, four years old,
With her brows puckered down
   In a painstaking frown
Under her tresses of gold.

'Twas Sunday, and nurse coming
   Exclaimed in a tone of surprise:
"Don't you know it's a sin
   Any work to begin
On the day that the Lord sanctifies?"

Then, lifting her face like a rose,
   Thus answered this wise little tot:
"Now, don't you suppose
   The good Lord he knows
This little iron ain't hot?"

ELIZABETH W. BELLAMY

HOLIDAYS *

IF Dorothy her wish could speak
  She'd have her birthday every week.
Just think! And when the year is through,
Her age would gain by fifty-two!

If Harriet could have her way
It would be always Christmas day;
She wishes Santa Claus would come
And make her chimneypiece his home.

July the Fourth is Johnny's choice—
The time when all the boys rejoice;
But if that day was always here,
We'd soon be all burned up, I fear.

And merry old St. Valentine
Would be the choice of Angeline;
But ah! I know if that were so,
The postmen all on strike would go.

So don't you think perhaps it's best
For holidays, as well, to rest,
And be on hand with joy and cheer,
Just once in all the long, long year?

                              ROSE MILLS POWERS

HOLIDAY WEATHER †

"ROASTING!" cries the turkey;
  "Chili!" says the sauce;
"Freezing!" moans the ice cream,
  "Mild!" calls the cheese across.

---

* From *The St. Nicholas Book of Verse* published by the Century Company.

† From *The St. Nicholas Book of Verse* published by the Century Company.

"Frosting!" the cake declares it;
"Clear!" vows the jelly bright;
"Pouring!" the coffee gurgles.
Now which do you think is right?

PAULINE FRANCES CAMP

THE TEAPOT DRAGON

THERE'S a dragon on our teapot,
With a long and crinkly tail,
His claws are like a pincer bug
His wings are like a sail;

His tongue is always sticking out,
And so I used to think
He must be very hungry, or
He wanted tea to drink.

But once when Mother wasn't round
I dipped my fingers in,
And when I pulled them out I found
I'd blistered all the skin.

Now when I see the dragon crawl
Around our china pot,
I know he's burned his tongue because
The water is so hot.

RUPERT SARGENT HOLLAND

SEUMAS BEG*

A MAN was sitting underneath a tree
Outside the village, and he asked me what
Name was upon this place, and said that he
Was never here before. He told a lot
Of stories to me too. His nose was flat.

---

* From *Collected Poems* by James Stephens, by permission of the Macmillan Company.

I asked him how it happened, and he said
The first mate of the Mary Ann done that
With a marlin-spike one day, but he was dead,
And jolly good job too; and he'd have gone
A long way to have killed him, and he had
A gold ring in one ear; the other one
"Was bit off by a crocodile, bedad."
That's what he said. He taught me how to chew.
He was a real nice man. He liked me, too.

JAMES STEPHENS

EXPLORATION *

"MY nursie said, this afternoon,
   While playing on the sand,
That if I'd dig, and dig, and dig,
   I'd get to China Land.

So with my spoon and spade I dug
   Until my arm was lame,
And in the bottom of the hole
   A little water came.

So I'm afraid that maybe p'raps
   My shovel may have hit
Against a Chinese laundry tub,
   And made a leak in it.

MARY STREET WHITTEN

A MYSTERY

I PLAYED at being tall to-day,
   And practiced from a chair;
How *can* grown people *pick* up things?
I don't see how they dare!

ROSAMOND LANG

* From *Lyrics for Lads and Lasses* by Mary Street Whitten and Julian Street; copyright, 1927, by D. Appleton and Company.

A SURPRISE *

WHEN the donkey saw the zebra
    He began to switch his tail.
"Well, I never!" was his comment;
    "Here's a mule that's been to jail."

MALCOLM DOUGLAS

THE SHAVE STORE

YESTERDAY, papa says, "Will it behave,
    If I should take it while I get a shave?"
'N' I says "Yes," as loud as I could talk,
So me en he, we went out for a walk
Clear to the Shave Store. En then I sat there
En papa climbed up in a dentist's chair
En had a bib on. En the shave man took
En painted papa till he made him look
Like frostin' on a angel cake. Mm! he looked nice!
'N' I thought the man was goin' to cut a slice.
He took a knife en wiped en wiped it, but
He didn't hurt my papa. He just cut
The frostin' off his face en took another
Knife en wiped it on a piece o' luther
En painted papa more, en cut en cut,
En mussed his hair, en slapped his face en shut
The old knife up. En washed his face, he did
Like papa washes mine sometimes, en calls me "Kid."
En he put baby powder on him, too,
En smelled him up, en when he was all through,
The Shave Store man says, "Bye, young lady, when
You want another shave, just call again!"

EDMUND VANCE COOKE

* From *The St. Nicholas Book of Verse* published by the Century Company.

SUFFERING

I SAT down on a bumble bee
   In Mrs. Jackson's yard.
I sat down on a bumble bee:
The bee stung good and hard.

I sat down on a bumble bee
For just the briefest spell,
And I had only muslin on,
As any one could tell.

I sat down on a bumble bee,
But I arose again;
And now I know the tenseness of
Humiliating pain.

NATHALIA CRANE

WHEN MOTHER SCRUBS

WHEN mother scrubs us Sunday morn,
   There's lively times, you bet;
There's faces wry, with howl and cry
   To keep out of the wet.
There's argument and weak excuse
   And faces full forlorn
When mother scrubs and digs and rubs
   Us every Sunday morn.

When mother scrubs us, there's a glow
   Of white comes o'er the scene,
A shedding of the old, and new
   Comes where the old has been;
A shrinkage in more ways than one,
   A wish we'd never been born,
When mother scours with all her powers
   On every Sunday morn.

When mother scrubs us Sunday morn,
    She gets all out of breath;
She pants and sweats and sighs and frets
    And scrubs us 'most to death.
She scrubs our backs till they are sore,
    Till skin and flesh are gone,
Then wonders why we'd rather die
    Than wake on Sunday morn.

No wonder Billy Buzzey says
    That I'm a thin-skinned jay;
I've got to be, 'cuz ma, you see,
    Has scrubbed it all away.
Oh, won't we be a happy lot,
    The wildest ever born,
When we're too big for ma to dig
    And scrub on Sunday morn?

UNKNOWN

I'M GLAD

I'M glad the sky is painted blue,
    And the earth is painted green,
With such a lot of nice fresh air
    All sandwiched in between.

UNKNOWN

IF

IF all the world were apple pie,
    And all the sea were ink,
And all the trees were bread and cheese,
    What should we have to drink?

UNKNOWN

"JUST WATCH PAPA!" *

FOURTH JULY, it seems to me,
Ain't what it's bragged up to be;
'Specially for childrens who
Live with kin they're kinfolks to.
Them with mothers who—all day—
Only have one thing to say:
"Just watch papa!"

Father takes down from the shelf
Fireworks he has bought hisself.
Does we git to shoot a shot?
No-siree-bob! We does not!
We must sit back in th' door,
Mother sayin', as before:
"Just watch papa!"

Father shoots an' shoots away,
Like 'twas his holiday.
Oh, he has th' biggest fun,
Gittin' all his shootin' done!
Still, 'bout all we hear is this,
Spoke right out with emphasis:
"Just watch papa!"

Say, you bet when I get grown,
Have some childrens all my own,
I'll show them just how to do—
Like our country wants us to.
I'll let them have all th' fun—
Show them zac'ly how it's done:
"Just watch papa!"

WILLIAM HERSCHELL

* From *The Smile Bringer;* copyright 1919–1926. Used by special
permission of the publishers, The Bobbs-Merrill Company.

A LITTLE BOY'S POCKET

DO you know what's in my pottet?
   Such a lot of treasures in it!
Listen now while I bedin' it:
Such a lot of sings it holds,
And everysin' dat's in my pottet,
And when, and where, and how I dot it.
First of all, here's in my pottet
A beauty shell, I pit'd it up:
And here's the handle of a tup
That somebody has broked at tea;
The shell's a hole in it, you see:
Nobody knows dat I dot it,
I teep it safe here in my pottet.
And here's my ball too in my pottet,
And here's my pennies, one, two, free,
That Aunty Mary dave to me,
To-morrow day I'll buy a spade,
When I'm out walking with the maid;
I tant put that here in my pottet!
But I can use it when I've dot it.
Here's some more sings in my pottet,
Here's my lead, and here's my string;
And once I had an iron ring,
But through a hole it lost one day,
And this is what I always say—
A hole's the worst sing in a pottet,
Be sure and mend it when you've dot it.

UNKNOWN

ARITHMETIC

I'M glad I have a good-sized slate,
   With lots of room to calculate.
Bring on your sums! I'm ready now;
My slate is clean and I know how.
But don't you ask me to subtract;
I like to have my slate well packed;

And only two long rows, you know,
Make such a miserable show;
And, please, don't bring me sums to add;
Well, multiplying's just as bad;
And, say! I'd rather not divide—
Bring me something I haven't tried!

UNKNOWN

LULU'S COMPLAINT

I'SE a poor 'ittle sorrowful baby,
    For B'idget is 'way down 'tairs:
My titten has sc'atched my fin'er,
    And Dolly won't say her p'ayers.

I hain't seen my bootiful mamma
    Since ever so long ado;
An' I ain't her tunnin'est baby
    No londer, for B'idget says so.

Mamma dot anoder *new baby*,
    Dod dived it—He did—yes'erday;
An' it kies, it kies—oh! so defful!
    I wis' He would take it away.

I don't wan't no "sweet 'ittle sister";
    I want my dood mamma, I do;
I want her to tiss me and tiss me,
    An' tall me her p'ecious Lulu.

I dess my dear papa will b'in' me
    A 'ittle dood titten some day;
Here's nurse wid my mamma's new baby;
    I wis' she would tate it away.

Oh! oh! what tunnin' red fin'ers!
    It sees me 'ite out of its eyes;
I dess we will teep it and dive it
    Some can'y whenever it kies.

I dess I will dive it my dolly
    To play wid 'mos' every day;
An' I dess, I dess—Say, B'idget,
    Ask Dod not to tate it away.

UNKNOWN

I SAW A SHIP A-SAILING

I SAW a ship a-sailing,
    A-sailing on the sea;
And, oh! it was all laden
    With pretty things for thee!

There were comfits in the cabin,
    And apples in the hold;
The sails were made of silk,
    And the masts were made of gold,

The four-and-twenty sailors
    That stood between the decks,
Were four-and-twenty white mice,
    With chains about their necks,

The captain was a duck,
    With a packet on his back,
And when the ship began to move.
    The captain said, "Quack, quack!"

UNKNOWN

THE AMBITIOUS MOUSE

IF all the world were candy
    And the sky were frosted cake,
Oh, it would be a splendid job
    For a mouse to undertake!

To eat a path of sweetmeats
　　Through candy forest aisles—
Explore the land of Peppermint
　　Stretched out for miles and miles.

To gobble up a cloudlet,
　　A little cup-cake star,
To swim a lake of liquid sweet
　　With shores of chocolate bar.

But best of all the eating,
　　Would be the toothsome fat,
Triumphant hour of mouse desire,
　　To eat a candy cat!

JOHN FARRAR

THE WINDMILL

SAID a hazy little, mazy little, lazy little boy:
　　"To see the windmill working so must every one annoy;
It can be stopped, I'm sure it can, and so I'd like to know
What in the world can ever make a windmill want to go?"

Said a quizzy little, frizzy little, busy little girl:
"What can be more delightful than to see a windmill whirl?
It loves to go, I'm sure it does, and hates to hang ker-flop;
Now, what on earth can ever make a windmill want to
　　stop?"

UNKNOWN

A TEA PARTY

YOU see, merry Phillis, that dear little maid,
　　Has invited Belinda to tea;
Her nice little garden is shaded by trees—
　　What pleasanter place could there be?

There's a cake full of plums, there are strawberries too,
    And the table is set on the green;
I'm fond of a carpet all daisies and grass—
    Could a prettier picture be seen?

A blackbird (yes, blackbirds delight in warm weather),
    Is flitting from yonder high spray;
He sees the two little ones talking together—
    No wonder the blackbird is gay.

KATE GREENAWAY

FREDDIE AND THE CHERRY TREE

FREDDIE saw some fine ripe cherries
    Hanging on a cherry tree,
And he said, "You pretty cherries,
    Will you not come down to me?"

"Thank you kindly," said a cherry,
    "We would rather stay up here;
If we ventured down this morning,
    You would eat us up, I fear."

One, the finest of the cherries,
    Dangled from a slender twig.
"You are beautiful," said Freddie,
    "Red and ripe, and oh, how big!"

"Catch me," said the cherry, "catch me,
    Little master, if you can."
"I would catch you soon," said Freddie,
    "If I were a grown-up man."

Freddie jumped, and tried to reach it,
    Standing high upon his toes;
But the cherry bobbed about,
    And laughed, and tickled Freddie's nose.

"Never mind," said little Freddie,
  "I shall have them when it's right."
But a blackbird whistled boldly,
  "I shall eat them all to-night."

Ann Hawkshawe

A MODERN MIRACLE *

ONCE w'en I'm sick th' doctor come
    An' 'en I put my tongue 'way out,
An' he says, "H-m-m! Nurse, get me some
    Warm water, please." An' in about
A minute, w'y, she did an' 'en
    He put a glass thing into it
An' 'en he wiped it off again
    An' put it in my mouth a bit.

'En after w'ile he took it out
    An' held it up w'ere he could see,
An' 'en he says, "H-m-m! 'Ist about
    Too high a half of a degree."
An' 'en Ma asked him if I'm bad
    An' he says "Nope!" 'ist gruff an' cross
'An says "W'y you can't kill a lad,
    An' if you do it ain't much loss!"

An' 'en she's mad an' he 'ist bust
    Out laughin' an' he says, "Don't fret,
He's goin' t' be all right, I trust.
    W'y he ain't even half dead yet."
An' 'en he felt my pulse, 'at way,
    An' patted me upon my head
'An says, "There ain't no school to-day,
    'Cuz one of th' trustees is dead!"

---

* Taken by permission from *Boys and Girls*, by James W. Foley;
copyrighted by E. P. Dutton and Company.

An' my, I'm awful sorry w'en
  He told me that. An' 'en he said.
"He'll be all right by noon." An' 'en
  He went away. An' Ma says, "Ned,
How do you feel?" An' 'en, you know,
  Since Doctor told me that, somehow,
I'm awful sick a w'ile ago,
  But, my! I'm almost well right now!

JAMES W. FOLEY

SPECKLES

WE played a game the other day
  Called "Speckles, Blots, and Dots"—
We tried to name the mostest things
That had the mostest spots.

David named the bullfrog
And Sammy named the trout,
And Susie tried to name herself,
But we counted freckles out!

My Daddy was the winner.
We all began to laugh
'Cause Daddy named the *mostest* spots
When he named the giraffe!

RUTH COLLAT

BIRDS, BUGS AND BEASTS

THE COW

"PRETTY Moo Cow, will you tell
        Why you like the fields so well?
You never pluck the daisies white,
Nor look up to the sky so bright;
So tell me, Moo Cow, tell me true,
Are you happy when you moo?"

"I do not pluck the daisies white;
I care not for the sky so bright;
But all day long I lie and eat
Pleasant grass, so fresh and sweet—
Grass that makes nice milk for you;
So I am happy when I moo."

Mrs. Motherly

KINDNESS TO ANIMALS

LITTLE children, never give
        Pain to things that feel and live:
Let the gentle robin come
For the crumbs you save at home—
As his meat you throw along
He'll repay you with a song;
Never hurt the timid hare
Peeping from her green grass lair,
Let her come and sport and play
On the lawn at close of day;
The little lark goes soaring high
To the bright windows of the sky,
Singing as if 'twere always spring,
And fluttering on an untired wing—
Oh! let him sing his happy song,
Nor do these gentle creatures wrong.

Unknown

THE QUEER LITTLE HOUSE

THERE'S a queer little house,
  And it stands in the sun,
When the good mother calls
  The children all run.
While under her roof,
  They are cozy and warm,
Though the cold wind may whistle
  And bluster and storm.

In the daytime, this queer
  Little house moves away,
And the children run after it,
  Happy and gay;
But it comes back at night,
  And the children are fed,
And tucked up to sleep
  In a soft feather bed.

This queer little house
  Has no windows nor doors—
The roof has no shingles,
  The rooms have no floors—
No fireplace, chimney,
  Nor stove can you see,
Yet the children are cozy
  And warm as can be.

The story of this
  Funny house is all true,
I have seen it myself,
  And I think you have, too,
You can see it to-day,
  If you watch the old hen,
When her downy wings cover
  Her chickens again.

UNKNOWN

TWO QUESTIONS

SAID tender-hearted Daisy to naughty Pussy Gray,
"Suppose I were a fairy, O, tell me, pussy, pray,
If you, in fright, were flying from a fierce and hungry foe,
Should I my magic wand wave, and make him let you go?"
      Then Pussy Gray looked very wise
      And answered yes, with her bright eyes.

"Suppose a timid mousie should venture once to peep
Outside her quiet doorway, where, seeming fast asleep,
Is crouched a crafty pussy, just ready for a spring,
Should I my magic wand wave, and to mousie safety bring?"
      Then Pussy Gray closed her bright eyes
      And stupid looked, instead of wise.

"O, Pussy Gray," said Daisy; "I'm sure you did not hear
Quite all of my last question, or else, 'tis very clear
That you ignore its lesson, and do not mean to try
To do to those around you as you would be done by.
      Now, Pussy Gray, don't wink and blink;
      But tell me truly what you think."

                                        M. T. ROUSE

FABLE

THE mountain and the squirrel
      Had a quarrel,
And the former called the latter "Little Prig";
Bun replied,
"You are doubtless very big;
But all sorts of things and weather
Must be taken in together,
To make up a year
And a sphere.
And I think it no disgrace
To occupy my place.
If I'm not so large as you,
You are not so small as I,

And not half so spry.
I'll not deny you make
A very pretty squirrel track.
Talents differ; all is well and wisely put;
If I cannot carry forests on my back,
Neither can you crack a nut."

Ralph Waldo Emerson

LONG TIME AGO

ONCE there was a little kitty,
   White as the snow;
In a barn she used to frolic
   Long time ago.

In the barn a little mousie
   Ran to and fro;
For she heard the little kitty
   Long time ago.

Two black eyes had little kitty,
   Black as a sloe;
And they spied the little mousie
   Long time ago.

Four soft paws had little kitty,
   Paws soft as snow;
And they caught the little mousie
   Long time ago.

Nine pearl teeth had little kitty,
   All in a row;
And they bit the little mousie
   Long time ago.

When the teeth bit little mousie,
   Mousie cried out, "Oh!"
But she slipped away from kitty
   Long time ago.

Unknown

SOUR GRAPES

A FOX was trotting on one day,
　　And just above his head
He spied a vine of luscious grapes,
　　Rich, ripe, and purple-red;
Eager he tried to snatch the fruit,
　　But, ah! it was too high!

Poor Reynard had to give it up,
　　And, heaving a deep sigh,
He curl'd his nose and said, "Dear me!
　　I would not waste an hour
Upon such mean and common fruit—
　　I'm sure those grapes are sour!"
'Tis thus we often wish thro' life,
　　When seeking wealth and pow'r;
And when we fail, say, like the fox,
　　We're "sure the grapes are sour!"

UNKNOWN

HIDDY–DIDDY!

HIDDY-DIDDY! Hiddy-Diddy!—
　　Ten small chicks and one old biddy!
"Cluck!" says the Biddy, "cluck, cluck, cluck!
Scratch as I do!—try your luck!"

How the chickens, one and all,
Crowd around her at her call!
One chick, missing, peeps to say:
"Chirp, chirp, chirp!—I've lost my way!"

Shrill and shriller, comes the sound!
"Chirp! chirp! chirp!—I shall be drowned!"
Biddy clucks, and bustles quick—
"Where, oh, where's my little chick?"

Mister Rooster bustles, too,
Screaming, "Cock-a-doodle-doo!
Biddy, I just chanced to look,
And saw your bantling in the brook!"

"Gob!" shrieks Turkey, "gob, gob, gobble!
Mrs. Hen, you're in a hobble!
Why don't some one stir about,
And help your little chicken out?"

"Moo!" roars Sukey, "moo, moo, moo!
What is there that I can do?"
"Uff!" grunts Piggy, "uff, uff, uff!
Say you're sorry, that's enough."

"Quack!" says Ducky, "quack, quack, quack!
I have brought your chicken back!"
"Oh!" says Biddy, "cluck, cluck, cluck!
Thank you! thank you! Mrs. Duck!"

UNKNOWN

THE FAMILY CAT

I CAN fold up my claws
In my soft velvet paws,
And purr in the sun
Till the short day is done—
    For I am the family cat.
I can doze by the hour
In the vine-covered bower,
Winking and blinking,
Through sunshine and shower—
    For I am the family cat.

From gooseberry bush
Or where bright currants blush,
I may suddenly spring
For a bird on the wing;
Or dart up a tree,

If a brown nest I see,
And select a choice morsel
For dinner or tea;
And no one to blame me,
Berate me, or shame me—
   For I am the family cat.

In the cold winter night,
When the ground is all white,
And the icicles shine
In a long silver line,
I stay not to shiver
In the moonbeam's pale quiver,
But curl up in the house
As snug as a mouse,

And play Jack Horner
In the cosiest corner;
Breaking nobody's laws,
With my chin on my paws,
Asleep with one eye, and
   Awake with the other
For pats from the children,
   Kind words from the mother—
   For I am the family cat.

UNKNOWN

THE HENS *

THE night was coming very fast;
It reached the gate as I ran past.

The pigeons had gone to the tower of the church
And all the hens were on their perch,

Up in the barn, and I thought I heard
A piece of a little purring word.

---

* From *Under the Tree* by Elizabeth Madox Roberts, New York:
The Viking Press. Copyright, 1922, by B. W. Huebsch, Inc.

I stopped inside, waiting and staying,
To try to hear what the hens were saying.

They were asking something, that was plain,
Asking it over and over again.

One of them moved and turned around,
Her feathers made a ruffled sound,

A ruffled sound, like a bushful of birds,
And she said her little asking words.

She pushed her head close into her wing,
But nothing answered anything.

ELIZABETH MADOX ROBERTS

THE SQUIRREL

"THE squirrel is happy, the squirrel is gay,"
    Little Henry exclaim'd to his brother;
"He has nothing to do or to think of but play,
    And to jump from one bough to another."

But William was older and wiser, and knew
    That all play and no work would not answer,
So he ask'd what the squirrel in winter must do,
    If he spent all the summer a dancer.

"The squirrel, dear Harry, is merry and wise,
    For true wisdom and mirth go together;
He lays up in summer his winter supplies,
    And then he don't mind the cold weather."

BERNARD BARTON

PUSSYCAT

PUSSYCAT lives in the servants' hall.
    She can set up her back and purr:
The little mice live in a crack in the wall,
    But they hardly dare venture to stir.

For whenever they think of taking the air,
    Or filling their little maws,
The pussycat says, "Come out if you dare;
    I will catch you all with my claws."

Scrabble, scrabble, scrabble! went all the little mice,
    For they smelt the Cheshire cheese;
The pussycat said, "It smells very nice,
    Now *do* come out if you please."

"Squeak!" said the little mouse, "Squeak, squeak, squeak!"
    Said all the young ones too,
"We never creep out when cats are about,
    Because we're afraid of *you*."

So the cunning old cat lay down on a mat,
    By the fire in the servants' hall:
"If the little mice peep out they'll think I'm asleep";
    So she rolled herself up like a ball.

"Squeak!" said the little mouse, "we'll creep out
    And eat some Cheshire cheese;
That silly old cat is asleep on the mat,
    And we may sup at our ease."

Nibble, nibble, nibble! went all the little mice,
    And they licked their little paws;
Then the cunning old cat sprang up from the mat,
    And caught them all with her claws.

Ann Hawkshawe

A CAT TO HER KITTENS

LITTLE kittens, be quiet—be quiet, I say!
    You see I am not in the humor for play.
I've watched a long time every crack in the house,
Without being able to catch you a mouse.

"Now, Muff, I desire you will let my foot go;
And, Prinny, how can you keep jumping, miss, so?

"Little Tiny, get up, and stand on your feet,
And be, if you can, a little discreet!
Am I to be worried and harass'd by you,
Till I really don't know what to think or to do?

"But hush! hush! this minute! now don't mew and cry—
My anger is cooling, and soon will pass by,
So kiss me and come and sit down on the mat,
And make your dear mother a nice happy cat."

ELIZA GROVE

THE GREEDY PIGGY THAT ATE TOO FAST

"OH, Piggy, what was in your trough
That thus you raise your head and cough?
Was it a rough, a crooked bone,
That cooky in the pail had thrown?
Speak, Piggy, speak! and tell me plain
What 'tis that seems to cause you pain."

"Oh, thank you, sir! I will speak out
As soon as I can clear my throat.
This morning, when I left my sty,
So eager for my food was I,
That I began my rich repast—
I blush to own it—rather fast;
And, what with haste, sir, and ill-luck,
A something in my poor throat stuck,
Which I discover'd very soon
To be a silver tablespoon.
This, sir, is all—no other tale
Have I against the kitchen pail."

"I hope it is; but I must own
I'm sorry for my tablespoon;
And scarcely can I overlook

The carelessness of Mistress Cook.
But, Piggy, profit by your pain,
And do not eat so fast again."

ELIZA GROVE

THE MILK JUG

(THE KITTEN SPEAKS)

THE Gentle Milk Jug blue and white
I love with all my soul;
She pours herself with all her might
To fill my breakfast bowl.

All day she sits upon the shelf,
She does not jump or climb—
She only waits to pour herself
When 'tis my supper time.

And when the Jug is empty quite,
I shall not mew in vain,
The Friendly Cow, all red and white,
Will fill her up again.

OLIVER HERFORD

A COW AT SULLINGTON

SHE leaves the puddle where she drinks,
And comes toward the roadway bar
And looks into our eyes, and thinks
What curious animals we are!

CHARLES DALMON

THE COW

THANK you, pretty cow, that made
Pleasant milk to soak my bread,
Every day, and every night,
Warm, and fresh, and sweet, and white.

Do not chew the hemlock rank,
Growing on the weedy bank;
But the yellow cowslips eat,
They will make it very sweet.

Where the purple violet grows,
Where the bubbling water flows,
Where the grass is fresh and fine
Pretty cow, go there and dine.

JANE AND ANN TAYLOR

"I HAD A LITTLE DOGGY"

I HAD a little Doggy that used to sit and beg;
But Doggy tumbled down the stairs and broke his little
    leg.
Oh! Doggy, I will nurse you, and try to make you well,
And you shall have a collar with a little silver bell.

Ah! Doggy, don't you think that you should very faithful
    be,
For having such a loving friend to comfort you as me?
And when your leg is better, and you can run and play,
We'll have a scamper in the fields and see them making hay.

But, Doggy, you must promise (and mind your word you
    keep)
Not once to tease the little lambs, or run among the sheep;
And then the little yellow chicks that play upon the grass,
You must not even wag your tail to scare them as you pass.

UNKNOWN

TO ONE CHOOSING A KITTEN

A BLACK-NOSED kitten will slumber all the day;
A white-nosed kitten is ever glad to play;
A yellow-nosed kitten will answer to your call;
And a gray-nosed kitten I wouldn't have at all.

UNKNOWN

THE RABBIT *

W HEN they said the time to hide was mine,
    I hid back under a thick grapevine.

And while I was still for the time to pass,
A little gray thing came out of the grass.

He hopped his way through the melon bed
And sat down close by a cabbage head.

He sat down close where I could see,
And his big still eyes looked hard at me,

His big eyes bursting out of the rim,
And I looked back very hard at him.

ELIZABETH MADOX ROBERTS

THE LAMB

L ITTLE lamb, who made thee?
    Dost thou know who made thee,
Gave thee life, and bade thee feed
By the stream and o'er the mead;
Gave thee clothing of delight,
Softest clothing, woolly, bright;
Gave thee such a tender voice,
Making all the vales rejoice?
  Little lamb, who made thee?
  Dost thou know who made thee?

  Little lamb, I'll tell thee;
  Little lamb, I'll tell thee;
He is callèd by thy name,
For He calls Himself a lamb;
He is meek and He is mild,

He became a little child.
I a child and thou a lamb,
We are callèd by His name.
    Little lamb, God bless thee!
    Little lamb, God bless thee!

WILLIAM BLAKE

SUMMER EVENING *

THE sandy cat by the Farmer's chair
    Mews at his knee for dainty fare;
Old Rover in his moss-greened house
Mumbles a bone, and barks at a mouse;
In the dewy fields the cattle lie
Chewing the cud 'neath a fading sky;
Dobbin at manger pulls his hay:
Gone is another summer's day.

WALTER DE LA MARE

I MET A LITTLE PUSSYCAT

I MET a little pussycat, and I said: "How-de-do?"
And all the pussycat would say was: "Me-ew, me-ew,
    me-ew!"
"All right," says I to pussycat: "I'll say good day to you."
But pussy only answered: "Me-ew, me-ew, me-ew!"

G. G. WIEDERSEIM

THE SPIDER AND THE FLY

"WILL you walk into my parlor?" said the Spider to
    the Fly—
" 'Tis the prettiest little parlor that ever you did spy;
The way into my parlor is up a winding stair,
And I have many curious things to show you when you're
    there."

---

* From *Peacock Pie* by Walter de la Mare, by permission of
Henry Holt and Company.

"Oh, no, no," said the little Fly, "to ask me is in vain,
For who goes up your winding stair can ne'er come down
    again."
"I'm sure you must be weary, dear, with soaring up so high;
Will you rest upon my little bed?" said the Spider to the
    Fly.
"There are pretty curtains drawn around, the sheets are fine
    and then,
And if you like to rest a while, I'll snugly tuck you in!"
"Oh, no, no," said the little Fly, "for I've often heard it
    said,
They never, never wake again, who sleep upon your bed!"

Said the cunning Spider to the Fly: "Dear friend, what can
    I do
To prove the warm affection I've always felt for you?
I have, within my pantry, good store of all that's nice;
I'm sure you're very welcome—will you please to take a
    slice?"
"Oh, no, no," said the little Fly; "kind sir, that cannot be,
I've heard what's in your pantry, and I do not wish to see!"
"Sweet creature," said the Spider, "you're witty and you're
    wise;
How handsome are your gauzy wings, how brilliant are
    your eyes!
I have a little looking-glass upon my parlor shelf,
If you'll step in one moment, dear, you shall behold
    yourself."
"I thank you, gentle sir," she said, "for what you're pleased
    to say,
And bidding you good morning now, I'll call another day."

The Spider turned him round about, and went into his den,
For well he knew the silly Fly would soon come back again;
So he wove a subtle web, in a little corner sly,
And set his table ready, to dine upon the Fly.
Then he came out of his door again, and merrily did sing—
"Come hither, hither, pretty Fly, with the pearl and silver
    wing;
Your robes are green and purple, there's a crest upon your
    head;

Your eyes are like the diamond bright, but mine are dull
    as lead!"

Alas, alas! how very soon this silly little Fly,
Hearing his wily, flattering words, came slowly flitting by:
With buzzing wings she hung aloft, then near and nearer
    drew—
Thinking only of her brilliant eyes, and green and purple
    hue,
Thinking only of her crested head—poor foolish thing! At
    last,
Up jumped the cunning Spider, and fiercely held her fast;
He dragged her up his winding stair, into his dismal den,
Within his little parlor—but she ne'er came out again!

And now, dear little children, who may this story read,
To idle, silly, flattering words, I pray you ne'er give heed:
Unto an evil counselor close heart, and ear, and eye,
And take a lesson from this tale, of the Spider and the Fly.

MARY HOWITT

MISTER FLY

WHAT a sharp little fellow is Mister Fly,
    He goes where he pleases, low and high,
And can walk just as well with his feet to the sky
    As I can on the floor;
    At the window he comes
    With a buzz and a roar,
    And o'er the smooth glass
    Can easily pass
    Or through the keyhole of the door.
He eats the sugar and goes away,
Nor ever once asks what there is to pay;
And sometimes he crosses the teapot's steam,
And comes and plunges his head in the cream;
Then on the edge of the jug he stands,
And cleans his wings with his feet and hands.
This done, through the window he hurries away,
And gives a buzz, as if to say,

"At present I haven't a minute to stay,
But I'll peep in again in the course of the day."
  Then again he'll fly
  Where the sunbeams lie,
  And neither stop to shake hands
  Nor bid good-by:
Such a strange little fellow is Master Fly,
Who goes where he pleases, low or high,
  And can walk on the ceiling
  Without ever feeling
A fear of tumbling down "sky high."

THOMAS MILLER

CHANTICLEER

O F all the birds from East to West
    That tuneful are and dear,
I love that farmyard bird the best,
  They call him Chanticleer.

Gold plume and copper plume,
  Comb of scarlet gay;
'Tis he that scatters night and gloom,
  And whistles back the day!

He is the sun's brave herald
  That, ringing his blithe horn,
Calls round a world dew-pearled
  The heavenly airs of morn.

O clear gold, shrill and bold!
  He calls through creeping mist
The mountains from the night and cold
  To rose and amethyst.

He sets the birds to singing,
  And calls the flowers to rise;
The morning cometh, bringing
  Sweet sleep to heavy eyes.

Gold plume and silver plume,
  Comb of coral gay;
'Tis he packs off the night and gloom,
  And summons home the day!

Black fear he sends it flying,
  Black care he drives afar;
And creeping shadows sighing
  Before the morning star.

The birds of all the forest
  Have dear and pleasant cheer,
But yet I hold the rarest
  The farmyard Chanticleer.

Red cock or black cock,
  Gold cock or white,
The flower of all the feathered flock,
  He whistles back the light.

KATHERINE TYNAN

CRADLE SONG

WHAT does little birdie say
  In her nest at peep of day?
Let me fly, says little birdie,
Mother, let me fly away.
Birdie, rest a little longer,
Till the little wings are stronger.
So she rests a little longer,
Then she flies away.

What does little baby say,
In her bed at peep of day?
Baby says, like little birdie,
Let me rise and fly away.
Baby, sleep a little longer,
Till the little limbs are stronger.
If she sleeps a little longer,
Baby too shall fly away.

LORD TENNYSON

THE GRASSHOPPER

THE Grasshopper, the Grasshopper,
     I will explain to you:—
He is the Brownies' racehorse,
     The fairies' Kangaroo.

VACHEL LINDSAY

ROBIN REDBREAST

LITTLE Robin Redbreast sat upon a tree,
     Up went pussycat, and down went he;
Down came pussycat, and away Robin ran;
Said little Robin Redbreast, "Catch me if you can."

Little Robin Redbreast jumped upon a wall,
Pussycat jumped after him, and almost got a fall;
Little Robin chirped and sang, and what did pussy say?
Pussycat said naught but "Mew," and Robin flew away.

UNKNOWN

THE EXAMPLE *

HERE'S an example from
     A Butterfly;
That on a rough, hard rock
     Happy can lie;
Friendless and all alone
On this unsweetened stone.

Now let my bed be hard,
     No care take I;
I'll make my joy like this
     Small Butterfly;
Whose happy heart has power
To make a stone a flower.

W. H. DAVIES

* Reprinted from the *Collected Poems* by W. H. Davies, through the courtesy of Alfred A. Knopf, Inc.

BOB WHITE

THERE'S a plump little chap in a speckled coat,
And he sings on the zigzag rails remote,
Where he whistles at breezy, bracing morn,
When the buckwheat is ripe, and stacked is the corn,
"Bob White! Bob White! Bob White!"

Is he hailing some comrade as blithe as he?
Now I wonder where Robert White can be!
O'er the billows of gold and amber grain
There is no one in sight—but, hark again:
"Bob White! Bob White! Bob White!"

Ah! I see why he calls; in the stubble there
Hide his plump little wife and babies fair!
So contented is he, and so proud of the same,
That he wants all the world to know his name:
"Bob White! Bob White! Bob White!"

GEORGE COOPER

LITTLE SNAIL *

I SAW a little snail
Come down the garden walk.
He wagged his head this way . . . that way . . .
Like a clown in a circus.
He looked from side to side
As though he were from a different country.
I have always said he carries his house on his back . . .
To-day in the rain
I saw that it was his umbrella!

HILDA CONKLING

* Reprinted by permission from *Poems by a Little Girl* by Hilda Conkling; copyright, 1920, by Frederick A. Stokes Company.

GRASSHOPPER GREEN

GRASSHOPPER green is a comical chap;
 He lives on the best of fare.
Bright little trousers, jacket, and cap,
 These are his summer wear.
Out in the meadow he loves to go,
 Playing away in the sun;
It's hopperty, skipperty, high and low,
 Summer's the time for fun.

Grasshopper green has a quaint little house;
 It's under the hedge so gay.
Grandmother Spider, as still as a mouse,
 Watches him over the way.
Gladly he's calling the children, I know,
 Out in the beautiful sun;
It's hopperty, skipperty, high and low,
 Summer's the time for fun.

UNKNOWN

THE WREN AND THE HEN

SAID a very small wren
 To a very large hen:
"Pray, why do you make such a clatter?
I never could guess
Why an egg more or less
Should be thought so important a matter."

Then answered the hen
To the very small wren:
"If I laid such small eggs as you, madam,
I would not cluck loud,
Nor would I feel proud.
Look at these! How you'd crow if you had 'em!"

UNKNOWN

THE OWL AND THE PUSSYCAT

THE Owl and the Pussycat went to sea
    In a beautiful pea-green boat.
They took some honey, and plenty of money,
    Wrapped up in a five-pound note.
The Owl looked up to the stars above,
    And sang to a small guitar,
"O lovely Pussy! O Pussy, my love,
    What a beautiful Pussy you are,
            You are!
    What a beautiful Pussy you are!"

Pussy said to the Owl, "You elegant fowl!
    How charmingly sweet you sing!
O let us be married! Too long we have tarried:
    But what shall we do for a ring?"
They sailed away for a year and a day,
    To the land where the Bong-tree grows,
And there in a wood a Piggy-wig stood,
    With a ring at the end of his nose,
            His nose,
    With a ring at the end of his nose.

"Dear Pig, are you willing to sell for one shilling
    Your ring?" Said the Piggy, "I will."
So they took it away, and were married next day
    By the Turkey who lives on the hill.
They dined on mince and slices of quince,
    Which they ate with a runcible spoon;
And hand in hand, on the edge of the sand,
    They danced by the light of the moon,
            The moon,
    They danced by the light of the moon.

                                EDWARD LEAR

BUTTERFLY *

BUTTERFLY,
  I like the way you wear your wings.
Show me their colors,
For the light is going.
Spread out their edges of gold,
Before the Sandman puts me to sleep
And evening murmurs by.

HILDA CONKLING

FIREFLIES

LITTLE lamps of the dusk.
  You fly low and gold
When the summer evening
  Starts to unfold,
So that all the insects,
  Now, before you pass,
Will have light to see by
  Undressing in the grass.

But when night has flowered
  Little lamps a-gleam,
You fly over tree tops
  Following a dream.
Men wonder from their windows
  That a firefly goes so far—
They do not know your longing
  To be a shooting star.

CAROLYN HALL

DREAMS

I SING of a dog, the dearest dog
  That ever teased a shoe;
His ears were straight, and his eyes were bright,
And filled with an impish heathen light;
  I loved him, and he loved me true.

We played together, Dreams and I,
  We ran at a leaping pace,
We laughed and barked in the summer sun,
And I slept on the hill when the play was done
  And Dreams had won the race.

And after the breeze had cooled my cheek,
  And the summer sounds had sung
And hummed and rustled a lullaby,
I woke with a yawn and a happy sigh
  At the touch of a rough warm tongue.

Ah, Dreams, you were ever so real to me,
  And I was glad and sad
To look down into the eyes of you—
So deep, so deep, for the size of you,
  Dear dog that I never had.

S. Virginia Sherwood

I'D RATHER BE ME

A PUSSYCAT can lap and smack
  And crawl, 'n' yawn and stretch its back,
Scratch the rugs and mew, mew, mew,
  And do all things that I can't do.
But then it can't wear pretty clothes,
  'N' it has whiskers near its nose;
It can't eat cake or drink pink tea—
  I guess I'd rather be just me!

Lilly Robinson

MY MOUSE

I LOVED to sit on the kitchen floor,
 And watch the hole so near the door,
Where sometimes came two eyes so black
 A-peeking through the little crack.
If I was still and did not squeak
 A mouse came out so still and meek.

Poor Mousie can come out no more—
They've closed the hole right near the door.

LILLY ROBINSON

QUESTIONS

I VISITED the animals,
 That live in our Zoo;
And there are lots of questions
I've saved to ask of you.

Why is the zebra's skin so tight?
The hippo's skin so loose?
Why does the old owl look so wise?
The peacock, such a goose?

What do the monkeys talk about
In their excited way?
I'm sure it would be lots of fun
If we knew what they say!

The turtle's house is fastened on
As tight as tight can be!
Are little boys as queer to them
As turtles are to me?

RUTH COLLAT

FLOWERS

WISHING

RING-TING! I wish I were a Primrose,
A bright yellow Primrose blowing in the Sprng!
The stooping boughs above me,
The wandering bee to love me,
The fern and moss to creep across,
And the Elm Tree for our King!

Nay—stay! I wish I were an Elm Tree,
A great lofty Elm Tree, with green leaves gay!
The winds would set them dancing,
The sun and moonshine glance in,
The birds would house among the boughs,
And sweetly sing!

O—no! I wish I were a Robin,
A Robin or a little Wren, everywhere to go;
Through forest, field, or garden,
And ask no leave or pardon,
Till Winter comes with icy thumbs
To ruffle up our wing!

Well tell! Where shall I fly to,
Where go to sleep in the dark wood or dell?
Before a day was over,
Home comes the rover,
For Mother's kiss—sweeter this
Than any other thing!

WILLIAM ALLINGHAM

FOUR-LEAF CLOVER

I KNOW a place where the sun is like gold
And the cherry blooms burst with snow,
And down underneath is the loveliest nook
Where the four-leaf clovers grow.

One leaf is for hope, and one is for faith,
  And one is for love, you know,
And God put another one in for luck;
  If you search you will find where they grow.

But you must have hope, and you must have faith,
  You must love and be strong, and so
If you work, if you wait, you will find the place
  Where the four-leaf clovers grow.

ELLA HIGGINSON

DAISIES

AT evening when I go to bed
    I see the stars shine overhead;
They are the little daisies white
That dot the meadow of the night.

And often while I'm dreaming so,
Across the sky the moon will go;
It is a lady, sweet and fair,
Who comes to gather daisies there.

For, when at morning I arise,
There's not a star left in the skies;
She's picked them all and dropped them down
Into the meadows of the town.

FRANK DEMPSTER SHERMAN

IN THE GARDEN

I SPIED beside the garden bed
    A tiny lass of ours,
Who stopped and bent her sunny head
  Above the red June flowers.

Pushing the leaves and thorns apart,
  She singled out a rose,
And in its inmost crimson heart,
  Enraptured, plunged her nose.

"O dear, dear rose, come, tell me true—
  Come, tell me true," said she,
"If I smell just as sweet to you
  As you smell sweet to me!"

ERNEST CROSBY

THE DAISY

I'M a pretty little thing,
  Always coming with the spring;
In the meadows green I'm found,
Peeping just above the ground;
And my stalk is covered flat
With a white and yellow hat.
Little lady, when you pass
Lightly o'er the tender grass,
Skip about, but do not tread
On my meek and lowly head;
For I always seem to say,
Surely winter's gone away.

UNKNOWN

BUTTERCUPS

THERE must be fairy miners
  Just underneath the mold,
Such wondrous quaint designers
  Who live in caves of gold.

They take the shining metals,
  And beat them into shreds;
And mold them into petals,
  To make the flowers' heads.

Sometimes they melt the flowers
  To tiny seeds like pearls,
And store them up in bowers
  For little boys and girls.

And still a tiny fan turns
  Above a forge of gold,
To keep, with fairy lanterns,
  The world from growing old.

WILFRED THORLEY

THE RHODORA

ON BEING ASKED WHENCE IS THE FLOWER

IN May, when sea winds pierced our solitudes,
  I found the fresh Rhodora in the woods,
Spreading its leafless blossoms in a damp nook,
To please the desert and the sluggish brook.
The purple petals, fallen in the pool,
Made the black water with their beauty gay;
Here might the redbird come his plumes to cool,
And court the flower that cheapens his array.
Rhodora! if the sages ask thee why
This charm is wasted on the earth and sky,
Tell them, dear, that if eyes were made for seeing,
Then Beauty is its own excuse for being:
Why thou wert there, O rival of the rose!
I never thought to ask, I never knew:
But, in my simple ignorance, suppose
The selfsame Power that brought me there brought you.

RALPH WALDO EMERSON

BABY SEED SONG

LITTLE brown brother, oh! little brown brother,
  Are you awake in the dark?
Here we lie cosily, close to each other.
Hark to the song of the lark.
"Waken," the lark says, "waken and dress you;
Put on your green coats and gay,
Blue sky will shine on you, sunshine caress you—
Waken! 'tis morning—'tis May!"

Little brown brother, oh! little brown brother,
What kind of flower will you be?
I'll be a poppy—all white, like my mother;
Do be a poppy like me.
What! you're a sunflower? How I shall miss you
When you're grown golden and high.
But I shall send all the bees up to kiss you;
Little brown brother, good-by.

EDITH NESBIT

DANDELION *

O LITTLE soldier with the golden helmet,
　What are you guarding on my lawn?
You with your green gun
And your yellow beard,
Why do you stand so stiff?
There is only the grass to fight!

HILDA CONKLING

* Reprinted by permission from *Poems by a Little Girl* by Hilda Conkling; copyright, 1920, by Frederick A. Stokes Company.

GOD'S WORLD

TO-DAY

SO here hath been dawning
  Another blue Day:
Think, wilt thou let it
  Slip useless away?

Out of Eternity
  This new Day is born;
Into Eternity,
  At night, will return.

Behold it aforetime
  No eye ever did:
So soon it forever
  From all eyes is hid.

Here hath been dawning
  Another blue Day:
Think, wilt thou let it
  Slip useless away?

Thomas Carlyle

THE WORLD'S MUSIC

THE world's a very happy place,
  Where every child should dance and sing,
And always have a smiling face,
  And never sulk for anything.

I waken when the morning's come,
  And feel the air and light alive
With strange sweet music like the hum
  Of bees about their busy hive.

The linnets play among the leaves
  At hide and seek, and chirp and sing;
While, flashing to and from the eaves,
  The swallows twitter on the wing.

And twigs that shake, and boughs that sway,
  And tall old trees you could not climb,
And winds that come, but cannot stay,
  Are singing gayly all the time.

From dawn to dark the old mill wheel
  Makes music, going round and round;
And dusty-white with flour and meal,
  The miller whistles to its sound.

The brook that flows beside the mill,
  As happy as a brook can be,
Goes singing its own song until
  It learns the singing of the sea.

For every wave upon the sands
  Sings songs you never tire to hear,
Of laden ships from sunny lands
  Where it is summer all the year.

And if you listen to the rain
  When leaves and birds and bees are dumb,
You hear it pattering on the pane
  Like Andrew beating on his drum.

The coals beneath the kettle croon,
  And clap their hands and dance in glee;
And even the kettle hums a tune
  To tell you when it's time for tea.

The world is such a happy place
  That children, whether big or small,
Should always have a smiling face
  And never, never sulk at all.

GABRIEL SETOUN

THE PASTURE *

I'M going out to clean the pasture spring;
I'll only stop to rake the leaves away
(And wait to watch the water clear, I may):
I sha'n't be gone long.—You come too.

I'm going out to fetch the little calf
That's standing by the mother. It's so young,
It totters when she licks it with her tongue.
I sha'n't be gone long.—*You come too.*

ROBERT FROST

SPRING IS COMING

I AM coming, little maiden!
With the pleasant sunshine laden,
With the honey for the bee,
With the blossoms for the tree,
With the flower, and with the leaf—
Till I come the time is brief.

I am coming! I am coming!
Hark! the little bee is humming;
See! the lark is soaring high
In the bright and sunny sky;
And the gnats are on the wing,
Wheeling round in airy ring.
See! the yellow catkins cover
All the slender willows over;
And on banks of mossy green
Starlike primroses are seen,
And their clustering leaves below,
White and purple violets blow.

* From *North of Boston* by Robert Frost, by permission of Henry Holt and Company.

Hark! the newborn lambs are bleating
And the cawing rooks are meeting
In the elms—a noisy crowd!
All the birds are singing loud;
And the first white butterfly
In the sunshine dances by.

UNKNOWN

SEPTEMBER

THE goldenrod is yellow
    The corn is turning brown,
The trees in apple orchards
    With fruit are bending down.

The gentian's bluest fringes
    Are curling in the sun,
In dusky pods the milkweed
    Its hidden silk has spun.

The sedges flaunt their harvest
    In every meadow nook,
And asters by the brookside
    Make asters in the brook.

From dewy lanes at morning
    The grapes' sweet odors rise,
At noon the roads all flutter
    With golden butterflies.

By all these lovely tokens
    September days are here,
With summer's best of weather
    And autumn's best of cheer.

HELEN HUNT JACKSON

THE NEW MOON

DEAR mother, how pretty
      The moon looks to-night!
She was never so lovely before;
      Her two little horns
      Are so sharp and so bright,
I hope she'll not grow any more.

      If I were up there
      With you and my friends,
I'd rock in it nicely—you'd see,
      I'd sit in the middle
      And hold by both ends;
Oh, what a bright cradle 'twould be!

      I would call to the stars
      To keep out of the way,
Lest we should rock over their toes;
      And there I would rock
      Till the dawn of the day,
And see where the pretty moon goes.

      And there we would stay
      In the beautiful skies,
And through the bright clouds we would roam;
      We would see the sun set,
      And see the sun rise,
And on the next rainbow come home.

ELIZA L. C. FOLLEN

SNOWFLAKES

WHENEVER a snowflake leaves the sky
      It turns and turns to say "Good-by!
Good-by, dear cloud, so cool and gray!"
Then lightly travels on its way.

And when a snowflake finds a tree,
"Good day!" it says—"Good day to thee!
Thou art so bare and lonely, dear,
I'll rest and call my comrades here."

But when a snowflake, brave and meek,
Lights on a rosy maiden's cheek,
It starts—"How warm and soft the day!
'Tis summer!"—and it melts away.

MARY MAPES DODGE

WAITING TO GROW

LITTLE white snowdrops just waking up,
    Violet, daisy and sweet buttercup;
Think of the flowers that are under the snow,
            Waiting to grow!

And think of what hosts of queer little seeds
Of flowers and mosses, of fern and of weeds,
Are under the leaves and under the snow,
            Waiting to grow!

Think of the roots getting ready to sprout,
Reaching their slender brown fingers about
Under the ice and the leaves and the snow,
            Waiting to grow!

Only a month or a few weeks more,
Will they have to wait behind that door,
Listen and watch and wait below,
            Waiting to grow!

Nothing so small, and hidden so well,
That God will not find it, and presently tell
His sun where to shine, and His rain where to go,
            Helping them grow!

UNKNOWN

WEATHER WISDOM

A SUNSHINY shower
Won't last half an hour.

Rain before seven,
Fair by eleven.

The South wind brings wet weather,
The North wind wet and cold together;
The West wind always brings us rain,
The East wind blows it back again.

March winds and April showers
Bring forth May flowers.

Evening red and morning gray
Set the traveler on his way;
But evening gray and morning red
Bring the rain upon his head.

Rainbow at night is the sailor's delight;
Rainbow at morning, sailors, take warning.

If bees stay at home,
Rain will soon come;
If they fly away,
Fine will be the day.

When clouds appear like rocks and towers,
The earth's refreshed by frequent showers.

UNKNOWN

DAYS OF THE MONTH

THIRTY days has September,
April, June, and November;
All the rest have thirty-one;
February twenty-eight alone—
Save in leap year, at which time
February's days are twenty-nine.

UNKNOWN

APRIL *

THE roofs are shining from the rain,
    The sparrows twitter as they fly,
And with a windy April grace
    The little clouds go by.

Yet the back yards are bare and brown
    With only one unchanging tree—
I could not be so sure of Spring
    Save that it sings in me.

SARA TEASDALE

THUNDERSTORMS †

MY mind has thunderstorms,
    That brood for heavy hours:
Until they rain me words,
    My thoughts are drooping flowers
And sulking, silent birds.

Yet come, dark thunderstorms,
    And brood your heavy hours;
For when you rain me words,
    My thoughts are dancing flowers
And joyful singing birds.

W. H. DAVIES

A QUEER THING

OH, trouble is a thing which many people borrow,
    And the flight of time gives other folks some sorrow.
And it is a fact, my dear,
    Which to me seems very clear,
That *to-day* will be *yesterday, to-morrow.*

LOFTUS FRIZELLE

* From *Rivers to the Sea* by Sara Teasdale, by permission of the Macmillan Company.
* Reprinted from the *Collected Poems* by W. H. Davies, through the courtesy of Alfred A. Knopf, Inc.

"THE NIGHT WILL NEVER STAY" *

THE night will never stay,
    The night will still go by,
Though with a million stars
You pin it to the sky,
Though you bind it with the blowing wind
And buckle it with the moon,
The night will slip away
Like sorrow or a tune.

ELEANOR FARJEON

THE STAR

TWINKLE, twinkle, little star,
    How I wonder what you are,
Up above the world so high,
Like a diamond in the sky.

When the blazing sun is set,
And the grass with dew is wet,
Then you show your little light,
Twinkle, twinkle, all the night.

Then the traveler in the dark
Thanks you for your tiny spark,
He could not see where to go
If you did not twinkle so.

In the dark blue sky you keep,
And often through my curtains peep,
For you never shut your eye
Till the sun is in the sky.

As your bright and tiny spark
Lights the traveler in the dark,
Though I know not what you are,
Twinkle, twinkle, little star.

JANE TAYLOR

---

* Reprinted by permission of the publishers, E. P. Dutton and Company.

PLAYGROUNDS

IN summer I am very glad
  We children are so small,
For we can see a thousand things
  That men can't see at all.

They don't know much about the moss
  And all the stones they pass:
They never lie and play among
  The forests in the grass:

They walk about a long way off;
  And, when we're at the sea,
Let father stoop as best he can
  He can't find things like me.

But, when the snow is on the ground
  And all the puddles freeze,
I wish that I were very tall,
  High up above the trees.

LAURENCE ALMA-TADEMA

MOTHER MOON *

A LIE-AWAKE SONG

THE moonlight is shining
  So white through my window.
The moon has been walking
All night through the sky,
The way that my mother
Comes walking on tiptoe,
When I'm thinking how slowly
The dark's going by.

* From *Selected Lyrics* of Amelia Josephine Burr, copyright, 1927,
by George H. Doran Company, Publishers.

The Sun is the father,
The Moon is the mother,
And the Stars are the children
Awake in the night.
She stoops down to kiss them
And tuck in the covers,
And when she is going
She leaves them her light.

AMELIA JOSEPHINE BURR

PUTTING THE WORLD TO BED

THE little snow people are hurrying down
    From their home in the clouds overhead;
They are working as hard as ever they can,
    Putting the world to bed.

Every tree in a soft fleecy nightgown they clothe;
    Each part has its nightcap of white.
And o'er the cold ground a thick cover they spread
    Before they say good night.

And so they come eagerly sliding down,
    With a swift and silent tread,
Always as busy as busy can be,
    Putting the world to bed.

ESTHER W. BUXTON

SEA SHELL

SEA Shell, Sea Shell,
    Sing me a song, O please!
A song of ships, and sailormen,
    And parrots, and tropical trees,

Of islands lost in the Spanish Main
Which no man ever may find again,
Of fishes and corals under the waves,
And seahorses stabled in great green caves.

Sea Shell, Sea Shell,
Sing of the things you know so well.

AMY LOWELL

HAPPY WIND *

OH, happy wind, how sweet
    Thy life must be!
The great, proud fields of gold
    Run after thee:
And here are flowers, with heads
    To nod and shake;
And dreaming butterflies
    To tease and wake.
Oh, happy wind, I say,
To be alive this day.

W. H. DAVIES

"WHO HAS SEEN THE WIND?"

WHO has seen the wind?
    Neither I nor you:
But when the leaves hang trembling,
    The wind is passing through.

Who has seen the wind?
    Neither you nor I:
But when the trees bow down their heads,
    The wind is passing by.

CHRISTINA GEORGINA ROSSETTI

---

* Reprinted from the *Collected Poems* by W. H. Davies, through
the courtesy of Alfred A. Knopf, Inc.

PENCIL AND PAINT *

WINTER has a pencil
    For pictures clear and neat,
She traces the black tree tops
Upon a snowy sheet.
But autumn has a palette
And a painting brush instead,
And daubs the leaves for pleasure
With yellow, brown, and red.

ELEANOR FARJEON

FOR A DEWDROP †

SMALL shining drop, no lady's ring
    Holds so beautiful a thing.
At sun-up in the early air
The sweetness of the world you snare.
Within your little mirror lie
The green grass and the wingèd fly;
The lowest flower, the tallest tree
In your crystal I can see.
Why, in your tiny globe you hold
The sun himself, a midge of gold.
It makes me wonder if the world
In which so many things are curled,
The world which all men real call,
Is not the real world at all,
But just a drop of dew instead
Swinging on a spider's thread.

ELEANOR FARJEON

WHO LIKES THE RAIN?

"I," SAID the duck. "I call it fun,
  For I have my pretty red rubbers on;
They make a little three-toed track,
In the soft, cool mud—quack! quack!"

"I!" cried the dandelion, "I!
My roots are thirsty, my buds are dry."
And she lifted a towsled yellow head
Out of her green and grassy bed.

"I hope 'twill pour! I hope 'twill pour!"
Purred the tree toad at his gray bark door,
"For, with a broad leaf for a roof,
I am perfectly weatherproof."

Sang the brook: "I laugh at every drop,
And wish they never need to stop
Till a big, big river I grew to be,
And could find my way to the sea."

"I," shouted Ted, "for I can run,
With my high-top boots and raincoat on,
Through every puddle and runlet and pool
I find on the road to school."

CLARA DOTY BATES

RAIN IN SPRING

SO soft and gentle falls the rain,
  You cannot hear it on the pain;
For if it came in pelting showers,
'Twould hurt the budding leaves and flowers.

GABRIEL SETOUN

SNOW

O COME to the garden, dear brother, and see,
What mischief was done in the night;
The snow has quite covered the nice apple tree,
And the bushes are sprinkled with white.

The spring in the grove is beginning to freeze,
The pond is hard frozen all o'er;
Long icicles hang in bright rows from the trees,
And drop in odd shapes from the door.

The old mossy thatch, and the meadows so green,
Are covered all over with white;
The snowdrop and crocus no more can be seen,
The thick snow has covered them quite.

And see the poor birds how they fly to and fro,
They're come for their breakfast again;
But the little worms all are hid under the snow,
They hop about chirping in vain.

Then open the window, I'll throw them some bread,
I've some of my breakfast to spare:
I wish they would come to my hand to be fed,
But they're all flown away, I declare.

Nay, now, pretty birds, don't be frightened, I pray,
You shall not be hurt, I'll engage;
I'm not come to catch you and force you away,
And fasten you up in a cage.

I wish you could know you've no cause for alarm,
From me you have nothing to fear;
Why, my little fingers could do you no harm,
Although you came ever so near.

JANE TAYLOR

A SPRING LILT

THROUGH the silver mist
　　Of the blossom spray
Trill the orioles: list
　　To their joyous lay!
"What in all the world, in all the world," they say,
"Is half so sweet, so sweet, is half so sweet as May?"

　　"June! June! June!"
　　Low croon
The brown bees in the clover.
　　"Sweet! sweet! sweet!"
　　Repeat
The robins, nested over.

UNKNOWN

THE SUN

SOMEWHERE it is always light;
　　For when 'tis morning here,
In some far distant land 'tis night,
　　And the bright moon shines there.

When you're undressed and going to bed,
　　They are just rising there,
And morning on the hills doth spread
　　When it is evening here.

And other distant lands there be,
　　Where it is always night;
For weeks and weeks they never see
　　The sun, nor have they light.

For it is dark both night and day,
　　But what's as wondrous quite,
The darkness it doth pass away,
　　And then for weeks 'tis light.

Yes, while you sleep the sun shines bright,
　　The sky is blue and clear;
For weeks and weeks there is no night,
　　But always daylight there.

THOMAS MILLER

THE SNOW MAN

A SNOW MAN stands in the moonlight gold
　　Smoking his pipe serenely,
For what cares he that the night is cold,
Though his coat is thin and his hat is old
　　And the blustering winds blow keenly.

He has heard the children telling in glee
　　That Santa Claus would visit
This night their beautiful Christmas tree;
And it is not strange he should wish to see
　　How this can happen—now is it?

UNKNOWN

A SONG OF TO-MORROW *

LI'L bit er trouble,
　　Honey, fer terday;
Yander come Termorrer—
　　Shine it all away!

Rainy Sky is sayin',
　　"Dis'll never do!
Fetch dem rainbow ribbons,
　　En I'll dress in blue!"

FRANK L. STANTON

---

* From *Up from Georgia* by Frank L. Stanton; copyright, 1902, by D. Appleton and Company.

LAUGHING SONG

WHEN the green woods laugh with the voice of joy,
  And the dimpling stream runs laughing by,
When the air does laugh with our merry wit,
And the green hill laughs with the noise of it;

When the meadows laugh with lively green,
And the grasshopper laughs in the merry scene,
When Mary and Susan and Emily
With their sweet round mouths sing Ha, ha, he!

When the painted birds laugh in the shade,
When our table with cherries and nuts is spread,
Come live and be happy and join with me
To sing the sweet chorus of Ha, ha, he!

WILLIAM BLAKE

THE EVENING STAR

THE evening star a child espied,
  The one star in the sky.
"Is that God's service flag?" he cried,
  And waited for reply.

The mother paused a moment ere
  She told the little one—
"Yes, that is why the star is there!
  God gave His only Son!"

HAROLD SETON

SUN AND RAIN

IF all were rain and never sun,
  No bow could span the hill;
If all were sun and never rain,
  There'd be no rainbow still.

CHRISTINA GEORGINA ROSSETTI

JACK FROST

THE door was shut, as doors should be,
 Before you went to bed last night;
Yet Jack Frost has got in, you see,
 And left your window silver white.

He must have waited till you slept;
 And not a single word he spoke,
But penciled o'er the panes and crept
 Away again before you woke.

And now you cannot see the trees
 Nor fields that stretch beyond the lane;
But there are fairer things than these
 His fingers traced on every pane.

Rocks and castles towering high;
 Hills and dales and streams and fields;
And knights in armor riding by,
 With nodding plumes and shining shields.

And here are little boats, and there
 Big ships with sails spread to the breeze;
And yonder, palm trees waving fair
 On islands set in silver seas.

And butterflies with gauzy wings;
 And herds of cows and flocks of sheep;
And fruit and flowers and all the things
 You see when you are sound asleep.

For, creeping softly underneath
 The door when all the lights are out,
Jack Frost takes every breath you breathe
 And knows the things you think about.

He paints them on the windowpane
 In fairy lines with frozen steam;
And when you wake, you see again
 The lovely things you saw in dream.

GABRIEL SETOUN

"I WANDERED LONELY AS A CLOUD"

I WANDERED lonely as a cloud
That floats on high o'er vales and hills
When all at once I saw a crowd,
A host, of golden daffodils;
Beside the lake, beneath the trees,
Fluttering and dancing in the breeze

Continuous as the stars that shine
And twinkle in the Milky Way,
They stretched in never-ending line
Along the margin of a bay:
Ten thousand saw I at a glance,
Tossing their heads in sprightly dance.

The waves beside them danced; but they
Outdid the sparkling waves in glee:
A poet could not but be gay,
In such a jocund company:
I gazed—and gazed—but little thought
What wealth the show to me had brought:

For oft, when on my couch I lie
In vacant or in pensive mood,
They flash upon that inward eye
Which is the bliss of solitude;
And then my heart with pleasure fills,
And dances with the daffodils.

WILLIAM WORDSWORTH

PIPPA'S SONG

THE year's at the spring
And day's at the morn;
Morning's at seven;
The hillside's dew-pearled;

The lark's on the wing;
The snail's on the thorn;
God's in his heaven—
All's right with the world.

ROBERT BROWNING

LITTLE RAINDROPS

OH, where do you come from,
    You little drops of rain,
Pitter patter, pitter patter,
    Down the windowpane?

They won't let me walk,
    And they won't let me play,
And they won't let me go
    Out of doors at all to-day.

They put away my playthings
    Because I broke them all,
And then they locked up all my bricks,
    And took away my ball.

Tell me, little raindrops,
    Is that the way you play,
Pitter patter, pitter patter,
    All the rainy day?

They say I'm very naughty,
    But I've nothing else to do
But sit here at the window;
    I should like to play with you.

The little raindrops cannot speak,
    But "pitter, patter pat"
Means, "We can play on *this* side:
    Why can't you play on *that?*"

MRS..HAWKSHAW

SEA FEVER *

I MUST go down to the seas again, to the lonely sea and
  the sky,
And all I ask is a tall ship and a star to steer her by;
And the wheel's kick and the wind's song and the white
  sail's shaking,
And the gray mist on the sea's face, and a gray dawn
  breaking.

I must go down to the seas again, for the call of the running
  tide
Is a wild call and a clear call that may not be denied;
And all I ask is a windy day with the white clouds flying,
And the flung spray and the blown spume, and the seagulls
  crying.

I must go down to the seas again, to the vagrant gypsy life,
To the gull's way and the whale's way where the wind's like
  a whetted knife;
And all I ask is a merry yarn from a laughing fellow
  rover,
And quiet sleep and a sweet dream when the long trick's
  over.

JOHN MASEFIELD

MY PLAYMATE *

I KNOW a little wave,
  Its home is on the sea,
But often it has come
To shore, to play with me.

---

* From *Collected Poems* by John Masefield, by permission of the
Macmillan Company.

† From *Lyrics for Lads and Lasses* by Mary Street Whitten and
Julian Street; copyright, 1927, D. Appleton and Company.

It lends me pretty toys—
Bright pebbles, weeds, and shells,
When I dig holes in sand
It fills them up like wells.

This little wave and I
Have happy times together.
We play upon the sand
Each day in pleasant weather.

MARY STREET WHITTEN

DO YOU FEAR THE WIND?

DO you fear the force of the wind,
    The slash of the rain?
Go face them and fight them,
Be savage again.
Go hungry and cold like the wolf,
    Go wade like the crane:
The palms of your hands will thicken,
The skin of your cheek will tan,
You'll grow ragged and weary and swarthy,
    But you'll walk like a man!

HAMLIN GARLAND

APRIL RAIN

IT is not raining rain for me,
    It's raining daffodils;
In every dimpled drop I see
    Wild flowers on the hills.

The clouds of gray engulf the day
    And overwhelm the town;
It is not raining rain to me,
    It's raining roses down.

It is not raining rain to me,
But fields of clover bloom,
Where any buccaneering bee
Can find a bed and room.

A health unto the happy,
A fig for him who frets!
It is not raining rain to me,
It's raining violets.

ROBERT LOVEMAN

A BOY'S SONG

WHERE the pools are bright and deep,
Where the gray trout lies asleep,
Up the river and over the lea,
That's the way for Billy and me.

Where the blackbird sings the latest,
Where the hawthorn blooms the sweetest,
Where the nestlings chirp and flee,
That's the way for Billy and me.

Where the mowers mow the cleanest,
Where the hay lies thick and greenest,
There to track the homeward bee,
That's the way for Billy and me.

Where the hazel bank is steepest,
Where the shadow falls the deepest,
Where the clustering nuts fall free,
That's the way for Billy and me.

Why the boys should drive away
Little sweet maidens from the play,
Or love to banter and fight so well,
That's the thing I never could tell.

But this I know, I love to play
Through the meadow, among the hay;
Up the water and over the lea,
That's the way for Billy and me.

JAMES HOGG

A CHILD'S EVENSONG

THE sun is weary, for he ran
    So far and fast to-day;
The birds are weary, for who sang
    So many songs as they?
The bees and butterflies at last
    Are tired out, for just think too
How many gardens through the day
    Their little wings have fluttered through.
    And so, as all tired people do,
They've gone to lay their sleepy heads
Deep, deep in warm and happy beds.
The sun has shut his golden eye
And gone to sleep beneath the sky,
The birds and butterflies and bees
Have all crept into flowers and trees,
And all lie quiet, still as mice,
Till morning comes—like father's voice.

So Geoffrey, Owen, Phyllis, you
Must sleep away till morning too.
Close little eyes, down little heads,
And sleep—sleep—sleep in happy beds.

RICHARD LE GALLIENNE

THE CREATION

ALL things bright and beautiful,
    All creatures, great and small,
All things wise and wonderful,
    The Lord God made them all.

Each little flower that opens,
  Each little bird that sings,
He made their glowing colors,
  He made their tiny wings;

The rich man in his castle,
  The poor man at his gate,
God made them, high or lowly.
  And order'd their estate.

The purple-headed mountain,
  The river running by,
The sunset and the morning
  That brightens up the sky;

The cold wind in the winter,
  The pleasant summer sun,
The ripe fruits in the garden—
  He made them every one.

The tall trees in the greenwood,
  The meadows where we play,
The rushes by the water
  We gather every day;—

He gave us eyes to see them,
  And lips that we might tell
How great is God Almighty
  Who has made all things well!

Cecil Frances Alexander

THE GARDEN YEAR

JANUARY brings the snow,
  Makes our feet and fingers glow.

February brings the rain,
Thaws the frozen lake again.

March brings breezes, loud and shrill,
To stir the dancing daffodil.

April brings the primrose sweet,
Scatters daisies at our feet.

May brings flocks of pretty lambs
Skipping by their fleecy dams.

June brings tulips, lilies, roses,
Fills the children's hands with posies.

Hot July brings cooling showers,
Apricots, and gillyflowers.

August brings the sheaves of corn,
Then the harvest home is borne.

Warm September brings the fruit;
Sportsmen then begin to shoot.

Fresh October brings the pheasant;
Then to gather nuts is pleasant.

Dull November brings the blast;
Then the leaves are whirling fast.

Chill December brings the sleet,
Blazing fire, and Christmas treat.

SARA COLERIDGE

HOW THEY SLEEP

SOME things go to sleep in such a funny way:
Little birds stand on one leg and tuck their heads away;

Chickens do the same, standing on their perch;
Little mice lie soft and still as if they were in church;

Kittens curl up close in such a funny ball;
Horses hang their sleepy heads and stand still in a stall;

Sometimes dogs stretch out, or curl up in a heap;
Cows lie down upon their sides when they would go to sleep.

But little babies dear are snugly tucked in beds,
Warm with blankets, all so soft, and pillows for their heads.

Bird and beast and babe—I wonder which of all
Dream the dearest dreams that down from dreamland fall!

UNKNOWN

COME, LITTLE LEAVES

"COME, little leaves," said the wind one day.
       "Come over the meadows with me and play;
Put on your dresses of red and gold,
For summer is gone and the days grow cold."

Soon as the leaves heard the wind's loud call,
Down they came fluttering, one and all;
Over the brown fields they danced and flew,
Singing the sweet little song they knew.

"Cricket, good-by, we've been friends so long,
Little brook, sing us your farewell song;
Say you are sorry to see us go;
Ah, you will miss us, right well we know.

"Dear little lambs in your fleecy fold,
Mother will keep you from harm and cold;
Fondly we watched you in vale and glade,
Say, will you dream of our loving shade?"

Dancing and whirling, the little leaves went,
Winter had called them, and they were content;
Soon, fast asleep in their earthy beds,
The snow laid a coverlid over their heads.

GEORGE COOPER

DEEDS OF KINDNESS

SUPPOSE the little Cowslip
 Should hang its golden cup
And say, "I'm such a little flower
 I'd better not grow up!"
How many a weary traveler
 Would miss its fragrant smell,
How many a little child would grieve
 To lose it from the dell!

Suppose the glistening Dewdrop
 Upon the grass should say,
"What can a little dewdrop do?
 I'd better roll away!"
The blade on which it rested,
 Before the day was done,
Without a drop to moisten it,
 Would wither in the sun.

Suppose the little Breezes,
 Upon a summer's day,
Should think themselves too small to cool
 The traveler on his way:
Who would not miss the smallest
 And softest ones that blow,
And think they made a great mistake
 If they were acting so?

How many deeds of kindness
 A little child can do,
Although it has but little strength
 And little wisdom too!
It wants a loving spirit,
 Much more than strength, to prove
How many thinks a child may do
 For others by its love.

UNKNOWN

THE YOUNG MYSTIC *

WE sat together close and warm,
  My little tired boy and I—
Watching across the evening sky
The coming of the storm.

No rumbling rose, no thunders crashed,
  The west wind scarcely sang aloud;
  But from a huge and solid cloud
The summer lightnings flashed.

And then he whispered "Father, watch;
  I think God's going to light His moon—"
  "And when, my boy" . . . . "Oh, very soon.
I saw Him strike a match!"

LOUIS UNTERMEYER

FRIENDS

HOW good to lie a little while
  And look up through the tree!
The Sky is like a kind big smile
  Bent sweetly over me.

The Sunshine flickers through the lace
  Of leaves above my head;
And kisses me upon the face
  Like Mother, before bed.

The Wind comes stealing o'er the grass
  To whisper pretty things;
And though I cannot see him pass,
  I feel his careful wings.

---

* From *Challenge* by Louis Untermeyer, by permission of Harcourt, Brace and Company, Inc., holders of the copyright.

So many gentle Friends are near
  Whom one can scarcely see,
A child should never feel a fear,
  Whenever he may be.

ABBIE FARWELL BROWN

SOME LITTLE RULES

SOME little rules that are good to know:
  Shall I give them you? Get up with the sun,
Break your fast; your lessons review;
  What is well begun is almost done.

When you enter your class in your dress so neat,
  With your hair well brushed and your hands quite clean,
Turn to your teacher and sweetly greet—
  She'll think you a courteous child, I ween.

And sit in your seat like a quiet young mouse,
  With your eyes as bright and your ears as quick;
Not stiff as a poker, nor straight as a house,
  But ready to notice and swift to pick,

Every golden word which the teacher lets fall,
  Every bit of knowledge to you unknown,
In obedience prompt to her orders all,
  And never the work of the hour postpone.

UNKNOWN

LEISURE *

WHAT is this life if, full of care,
  We have no time to stand and stare.

No time to stand beneath the boughs
And stare as long as sheep or cows.

* Reprinted from the *Collected Poems* by W. H. Davies, through the courtesy of Alfred A. Knopf, Inc.

No time to see, when woods we pass,
Where squirrels hide their nuts in grass.

No time to see, in broad daylight,
Streams full of stars, like stars at night.

No time to turn at Beauty's glance,
And watch her feet, how they can dance.

No time to wait till her mouth can
Enrich that smile her eyes began.

A poor life this if, full of care,
We have no time to stand and stare.

W. H. DAVIES

THE NORTH WIND

SAID the wind one day,
"I am tired of play,
And I don't know where to blow.
Would the tall trees care,
If I should tear
Their leaves from the branches, so?"

Then the merry elf
Just helped himself
To the leaves, red, gold and brown;
While their cloud friends cried,
And in snowflakes died,
As the leaves fell fluttering down.

And the tall trees bare,
To and fro in the air,
Reached after their leaves, wind-tossed.
And they cannot forget—
They are reaching yet,
For leaves that the North Wind lost.

EILEEN WICKIZER

SONGS OF JOY

"ONLY A BABY SMALL"

ONLY a baby small,
   Dropped from the skies,
Only a laughing face,
   Two sunny eyes;
Only two cherry lips,
   One chubby nose;
Only two little hands,
   Ten little toes.

Only a golden head,
   Curly and soft;
Only a tongue that wags
   Lordly and oft;
Only a little brain,
   Empty of thought;
Only a little heart,
   Troubled with naught.

Only a tender flower
   Sent us to rear;
Only a life to love
   While we are here;
Only a baby small,
   Never at rest;
Small, but how dear to us,
   God knowest best.

MATTHIAS BARR

THE CRUST OF BREAD

I MUST not throw upon the floor
   The crust I cannot eat;
For many little hungry ones
   Would think it quite a treat.

My parents labor very hard
  To get me wholesome food;
Then I must never waste a bit
  That would do others good.

For willful waste makes woeful want,
  And I may live to say,
Oh! how I wish I had the bread
  That once I threw away!

UNKNOWN

BE TRUE

THOU must be true thyself
    If thou the truth wouldst teach;
Thy soul must overflow, if thou
  Another's soul wouldst reach!
It needs the overflow of heart
  To give the lips full speech.

Think truly, and thy thoughts
  Shall the world's famine feed;
Speak truly, and each word of thine
  Shall be a fruitful seed;
Live truly, and thy life shall be
  A great and noble creed.

HORATIO BONAR

TO A CHILD

SMALL service is true service while it lasts:
  Of humblest friends, bright creature! scorn not one:
The daisy, by the shadow that it casts,
Protects the lingering dewdrop from the sun.

WILLIAM WORDSWORTH

FOUR THINGS

FOUR things a man must learn to do
If he would make his record true:
To think without confusion clearly;
To love his fellow men sincerely;
To act from honest motives purely;
To trust in God and Heaven securely.

HENRY VAN DYKE

DUTY

SO nigh is grandeur to our dust,
So near is God to man,
When Duty whispers low, "Thou must,"
The youth replies, "I can."

RALPH WALDO EMERSON

WORK

NO man is born into the world whose work
Is not born with him; there is always work
And tools to work withal, for those who will,
And blessed are the horny hands of toil;
The busy world shoves angrily aside
The man who stands with arms akimbo set,
Until occasion tells him what to do;
And he who waits to have his task marked out,
Shall die and leave his errand unfulfilled.

JAMES RUSSELL LOWELL

DICK SAID: *

(CONCERNING HEAVEN)

WELL, Heaven's hard to understand—
But it's a kind of great, big land
All full of gold and glory;

---

* From *These Times* by Louis Untermeyer; by permission of Harcourt, Brace and Company, Inc., holders of the copyright.

With rivers green and pink and red,
And houses made of gingerbread
    Like in the fairy story.

The floors they use are made of clouds;
And there are crowds and crowds and crowds
    Who sing and dance till seven.
But then they must keep still because
God and the Dream Man and Santa Claus
    Sleep in the big House of Heaven.

God, He sleeps on the first two floors;
And the Dream Man sleeps above Him and snores,
    A tired-out story-teller;
And Santa Claus, who hates the noise,
He sleeps on the roof with all of his toys—
    And the angels live in the cellar.

Now, the angels never sleep a wink,
They're much too busy to stop and think
    Or play on harps and guitars.
They're always cleaning the sun at night,
And all day long, to keep them bright,
    They polish the moon and the stars.

They clean the streets and they tidy the rooms,
And they sweep out Heaven with a million brooms,
    And they hurry each other when they nod,
And they work so fast that they almost fall—
But God just sits and never works at all;
    And that's because He's God!

                              LOUIS UNTERMEYER

MY SHADOW

I HAVE a little shadow that goes in and out with me,
And what can be the use of him is more than I can see.
He is very, very like me from the heels up to the head;
And I see him jump before me, when I jump into my bed.

The funniest thing about him is the way he likes to grow—
Not at all like proper children, which is always very slow;
For he sometimes shoots up taller like an India-rubber ball,
And he sometimes gets so little that there's none of him at
    all.

He hasn't got a notion of how children ought to play,
And can only make a fool of me in every sort of way.
He stays so close beside me, he's a coward you can see;
I'd think shame to stick to nursie as that shadow sticks to
    me!

One morning, very early, before the sun was up,
I rose and found the shining dew on every buttercup;
But my lazy little shadow, like an arrant sleepyhead,
Had stayed at home behind me and was fast asleep in bed.

ROBERT LOUIS STEVENSON

EXTREMES *

A LITTLE boy once played so loud
    That the Thunder, up in a thundercloud,
Said, "Since *I* can't be heard, why, then,
I'll never, never thunder again!"

And a little girl once kept so still
That she heard a fly on the window sill
Whisper and say to a ladybird,
"She's the stilliest child I ever heard!"

JAMES WHITCOMB RILEY

THE MILL

WINDING and grinding
    Round goes the mill,
Winding and grinding
Should never stand still.

* From the *Book of Joyous Children*, copyright, 1902. Used by
special permission of the publishers, The Bobbs-Merrill Company.

Ask not your neighbor
Grind great or small,
Span not your labor,
Grind your wheat all.

DINAH MARIA MULOCK CRAIK

THE EFFECT OF EXAMPLE

WE scatter seeds with careless hand,
And dream we ne'er shall see them more;
But for a thousand years
Their fruit appears,
In weeds that mar the land,
Or healthful shore.

The deeds we do, the words we say—
Into still air they seem to fleet,
We count them ever past;
But they shall last—
In the dread judgment they
And we shall meet.

I charge thee by the years gone by,
For the love's sake of brethren dear,
Keep thou the one true way,
In work and play,
Lest in that world their cry
Of woe thou hear.

JOHN KEBLE

THE WAY

GOOD morrow, fair maid, with lashes brown.
Can you tell me the way to Womanhood town?
Oh! this way and that way—never stop,
'Tis picking up articles Grandma will drop,
'Tis kissing the baby's troubles away;
'Tis learning that cross words never will pay;

'Tis helping mother, 'tis sewing up rents;
'Tis reading and playing, 'tis saving cents;
'Tis loving and smiling, forgetting to frown:
Oh, that is the way to Womanhood town!

UNKNOWN

A CHILD'S THOUGHT OF GOD

THEY say that God lives very high!
But if you look above the pines
You cannot see our God. And why?

And if you dig down in the mines
You never see Him in the gold,
Though from Him all that's glory shines.

God is so good, He wears a fold
Of heaven and earth across His face—
Like secrets kept, for love untold.

But still I feel that His embrace
Slides down by thrills, through all things made,
Through sight and sound of every place:

As if my tender mother laid
On my shut lids, her kisses' pressure,
Half-waking me at night and said,
"Who kissed you through the dark, dear guesser?"

ELIZABETH BARRETT BROWNING

A FAREWELL

MY fairest child, I have no song to give you;
No lark could pipe to skies so dull and gray:
Yet, if you will, one quiet hint I'll leave you
For every day.

I'll tell you how to sing a clearer carol
   Than lark who hails the dawn on breezy down;
To earn yourself a purer poet's laurel
         Than Shakespeare's crown.

Be good, sweet maid, and let who will be clever;
   Do noble things, not dream them, all day long:
And so make Life, and Death, and that For Ever
         One grand sweet song

                                    CHARLES KINGSLEY

PATRIOTIC

PREAMBLE TO THE CONSTITUTION OF THE UNITED STATES OF AMERICA

WE, the people of the United States, in order to form a more perfect union, establish justice, insure domestic tranquillity, provide for the common defense, promote the general welfare, and secure the blessings of liberty to ourselves and our posterity, do ordain and establish this Constitution.

OUR NATIVE LAND

OTHER countries, far and near,
　　Other people hold most dear;
Other countries ne'er can be
Half so dear to you and me
As our own, our native land.
By it firmly let us stand.

C. PHILLIPS

IF EVER TIME SHALL COME

IF ever time shall come when I can see
　　A crimson cross against a field of white,
And fail to hear the words it speaks to me,
Lord, pierce my spirit with the sword of Light.

And let me glimpse the vision once again,
For Jesus' sake a cup of water given;
And in His name relief from weary pain,
And mercy, tender snowy-winged from Heaven.

And where it hovers o'er the battle line,
The symbol of a mighty mother's care,
May I not say the crimson cross is mine,
If I have helped to place its banner there?

ALISON BROWN

THE TORCH OF LIBERTY

I SAW it all in Fancy's glass—
  Herself, the fair, the wild magician,
Who bade this splendid daydream pass,
  And named this gilded apparition.
'Twas like a torch race—such as they
  Of Greece performed in ages gone,
When the fleet youths in long array,
  Passed the bright torch triumphant on,

To catch the coming flame in turn;
I saw the expectant nation and
  The clear, though struggling, glory burn.
And oh, their joy, as it came near,
  'Twas, in itself, a joy to see;
While Fancy whispered in my ear,
  "That torch they pass is Liberty!"

And each, as she received the flame,
  Lighted her altar with its ray;
Then, smiling, to the next who came,
  Speeded it on its sparkling way.
From Albion first, whose ancient shrine
  Was furnished with the flame already,
Columbia caught the boon divine,
  And lit a flame, like Albion's, steady.

Shine, shine forever, glorious flame,
  Divinest gift of gods to men!
From Greece thy earliest splendor came,
  To Greece thy ray returns again.
Take, Freedom, take thy radiant round;
  When dimmed, revive; when lost, return;
Till not a shrine through earth be found
  On which thy glories shall not burn!

THOMAS MOORE

THERE IS A LAND

THERE is a land, of every land the pride,
　　Beloved by Heaven o'er all the world beside;
Where brighter suns dispense serener light,
And milder moons imparadise the night;
A land of beauty, virtue, valor, truth,
Time-tutored age, and love-exalted youth.
Where shall that land, that spot of earth be found?
Art thou a man? a patriot? look around!
Oh! thou shalt find, howe'er thy footsteps roam,
That land thy country, and that spot thy home.

JAMES MONTGOMERY

A CREED

LORD, let me not in service lag,
　　Let me be worthy of our flag:
Let me remember, when I'm tried,
The sons heroic who have died
In freedom's name, and in my way
Teach me to be as brave as they.

In all I am, in all I do
Unto our flag I would be true;
For God and country let me stand.
Unstained of soul and clean of hand,
Teach me to serve and guard and love
The Starry Flag which flies above.

EDGAR A. GUEST

FOR THOSE WHO FAIL

"ALL honor to him who shall win the prize,"
　　The world has cried for a thousand years;
But to him who tries and who fails and dies,
　　I give great honor and glory and tears.

O great is the hero who wins a name,
But greater many and many a time
Some pale-faced fellow who dies in shame,
And lets God finish the thought sublime.

O great is the man with a sword undrawn,
And good is the man who refrains from wine;
But the man who fails and yet fights on,
Lo, he is the twin brother of mine!

JOAQUIN MILLER

DAYS WE CELEBRATE

LINCOLN'S BIRTHDAY
LINCOLN

I KNEW the man. I see him, as he stands
  With gifts of mercy in his outstretched hands;
A kindly light within his gentle eyes,
Sad as the toil in which his heart grew wise;
His lips half-parted with the constant smile
That kindled truth, but foiled the deepest guile;
His head bent forward, and his willing ear
Divinely patient right and wrong to hear:
Great in his goodness, humble in his state,
Firm in his purpose, yet not passionate,
He led his people with a tender hand,
And won by love a sway beyond command,
Summoned by lot to mitigate a time
Frenzied by rage, unscrupulous with crime,
He bore his mission with so meek a heart
That Heaven itself took up his people's part,
And when he faltered, helped him ere he fell,
Eking his efforts out by miracle.
No King this man, by grace of God's intent;
No, something better, freeman—President!
A nature, modeled on a higher plan,
Lord of himself, an inborn gentleman!

GEORGE HENRY BOKER

LINCOLN

WOULD I might rouse the Lincoln in you all,
  That which is gendered in the wilderness
From lonely prairies and God's tenderness.
Imperial soul, star of a weedy stream,
Born where the ghosts of buffaloes still dream,
Whose spirit hoof beats storm above his grave,
Above that breast of earth and prairie fire—
Fire that freed the slave.

VACHEL LINDSAY

ABRAHAM LINCOLN, THE MASTER

WE need him now—his rugged faith that held
 Fast to the rock of Truth through all the days
Of moil and strife, the sleepless nights; upheld
By very God was he—that God who stays
All hero souls who will but trust in Him,
And trusting, labor as if God were not.
His eyes beheld the stars, clouds could not dim
Their glory; but his task was not forgot—
To keep his people one; to hold them true
To that fair dream their fathers willed to them—
Freedom for all; to spur them; to renew
Their hopes in bitter days; strife to condemn.
Such was his task, and well his work was done—
Who willed us greater tasks, when set his sun.

THOMAS CURTIS CLARK

ABRAHAM LINCOLN

THIS man whose homely face you look upon,
 Was one of nature's masterful, great men;
Born with strong arms, that unfought battles won;
 Direct of speech, and cunning with the pen.
Chosen for large designs, he had the art
 Of winning with his humor, and he went
Straight to his mark, which was the human heart;
 Wise, too, for what he could not break he bent.

Upon his back a more than Atlas-load,
 The burden of the Commonwealth, was laid;
He stooped, and rose up to it, though the road
 Shot suddenly downwards, not a whit dismayed.
Hold, warriors, councilors, kings! All now give place
To this dear benefactor of the race.

RICHARD HENRY STODDARD

GEORGE WASHINGTON'S BIRTHDAY

GEORGE WASHINGTON

ONLY a baby, fair and small,
　　Like many another baby son,
Whose smiles and tears come swift at call;
Who ate, and slept, and grew, that's all—
　　The infant Washington.

Only a boy, like other boys,
　　With tasks and studies, sports and fun;
Fond of his books and games and toys;
Living his childish griefs and joys—
　　The little Washington.

Only a lad, awkward and shy,
　　Skilled in handling a horse or gun;
Mastering knowledge that, by and by,
Should aid him in duties great and high—
　　The youthful Washington.

Only a man of finest bent,
　　Hero of battles fought and won;
Surveyor, General, President,
Who served his country, and died content—
　　The patriot Washington.

Only—ah! what was the secret, then,
　　Of this being America's honored son?
Why was he famed above other men?
His name upon every tongue and pen—
　　The illustrious Washington.

A mighty brain, a will to endure,
　　Passions subdued, a slave to none,
A heart that was brave and strong and sure,
A soul that was noble and great and pure,
A faith in God that was held secure—
　　This was George Washington.

UNKNOWN

GEORGE WASHINGTON

THIS was the man God gave us when the hour
   Proclaimed the dawn of Liberty begun;
Who dared a deed, and died when it was done,
Patient in triumph, temperate in power—
Not striving like the Corsican to tower
To heaven, nor like great Philip's greater son
To win the world and weep for worlds unwon,
Or lose the star to revel in the flower.
The lives that serve the eternal verities
Alone do mold mankind. Pleasure and pride
Sparkle awhile and perish, as the spray
Smoking across the crests of the cavernous seas
Is impotent to hasten or delay
The everlasting surges of the tide.

John Hall Ingham

Arbor Day

CHILD'S SONG OF SPRING

THE silver birch is a dainty lady,
   She wears a satin gown;
The elm tree makes the old churchyard shady,
   She will not live in town.

The English oak is a sturdy fellow,
   He gets his green coat late;
The willow is smart in a suit of yellow,
   While brown the beech trees wait.

Such a gay green gown God gives the larches—
   As green as He is good!
The hazels hold up their arms for arches
   When Spring rides through the wood.

The chestnut's proud and the lilac's pretty,
   The poplar's gentle and tall,

E. Nesbit

But the plane tree's kind to the poor dull city—
   I love him best of all!

SONG

FOR the tender beech and the sapling oak,
   That grow by the shadowy rill,
You may cut down both at a single stroke,
   You may cut down which you will.

But this you must know, that as long as they grow,
   Whatever change may be,
You can never teach either oak or beech
   To be aught but a greenwood tree.

THOMAS LOVE PEACOCK

THE OAK

THE monarch oak, the patriarch of the trees,
   Shoots slowly up, and spreads by slow degrees;
Three centuries he grows, and three he stays
Supreme in state, and in three more decays.

JOHN DRYDEN

TREE PLANTING

OH happy trees that we plant to-day,
   What great good fortunes wait you!
For you will grow in sun and snow
   Till fruit and flowers freight you.

Your winter covering of snow
   Will dazzle with its splendor;
Your summer's garb with richest glow,
   Will feast of beauty render.

In your cool shade will tired feet
　　Pause, weary, when 'tis summer;
And rest like this will be most sweet
　　To every tired comer.

UNKNOWN

TREES

THE Oak is called the King of Trees,
　　The Aspen quivers in the breeze,
The Poplar grows up straight and tall,
The Pear Tree spreads along the wall,
The Sycamore gives pleasant shade,
The Willow droops in watery glade,
The Fir Tree useful timber gives,
The Beech amid the forest lives.

SARA COLERIDGE

AN ARBOR DAY TREE

DEAR little tree that we plant to-day,
　　What will you be when we're old and gray?
"The savings bank of the squirrel and mouse,
For robin and wren an apartment house,
The dressing room of the butterfly's ball,
The locust's and katydid's concert hall,
The schoolboy's ladder in pleasant June,
The schoolgirl's tent in the July noon,
And my leaves shall whisper them merrily
A tale of the children who planted me."

UNKNOWN

"WHAT DO WE PLANT?"

WHAT do we plant when we plant the tree?
　　We plant the ship, which will cross the sea.
We plant the mast to carry the sails;
We plant the planks to withstand the gales—

The keel, the keelson, the beam, the knee;
We plant the ship when we plant the tree.

What do we plant when we plant the tree?
We plant the houses for you and me.
We plant the rafters, the shingles, the floors,
We plant the studding, the lath, the doors,
The beams and siding, all parts that be;
We plant the house when we plant the tree.

What do we plant when we plant the tree?
A thousand things that we daily see;
We plant the spire that out-towers the crag,
We plant the staff for our country's flag,
We plant the shade, from the hot sun free;
We plant all these when we plant the tree.

HENRY ABBEY

THE TREE

THE tree's early leaf buds were bursting their brown:
"Shall I take them away?" said the frost, sweeping
down.
"No, dear; leave them alone
Till blossoms here have grown,"
Prayed the tree, while it trembled from rootlet to crown.

The tree bore its blossoms, and all the birds sung:
"Shall I take them away?" said the wind, as it swung.
"No, dear; leave them alone
Till berries here have grown,"
Said the tree, while its leaflets all quivering hung.

The tree bore its fruit in the midsummer glow:
Said the girl, "May I gather thy berries or no?"
"Yes, dear, all thou canst see;
Take them; all are for thee,"
Said the tree, while it bent its laden boughs low.

BJÖRNSTJERNE BJÖRNSON

AMONG THE NUTS

A WEE little nut lay deep in its nest
  Of satin and down, the softest and best;
And slept and grew, while its cradle rocked,
As it hung in the boughs that interlocked.

Now the house was small where the cradle lay,
As it swung in the wind by night and day;
For a thicket of underbrush fenced it round,
This little lone cot by the great sun browned.

The little nut grew, and ere long it found
There was work outside on the soft green ground;
It must do its part so the world might know
It had tried one little seed to sow.

And soon the house that had kept it warm
Was tossed about by the winter's storm;
The stem was cracked, the old house fell,
And the chestnut shell was an empty shell.

But the little seed, as it waiting lay,
Dreamed a wonderful dream from day to day,
Of how it should break its coat of brown,
And live as a tree to grow up and down.

UNKNOWN

ARMISTICE DAY

PEACE

WERE half the power that fills the world with terror,
  Were half the wealth bestowed on camps and courts,
Given to redeem the human mind from error,
  There were no need of arsenal or forts.
The warrior's name would be a name abhorrèd;
  And every nation that should lift again

Its hand against a brother, on its forehead
  Would wear forevermore the curse of Cain!
                                    HENRY WADSWORTH LONGFELLOW

RED CROSS DAY

THE LEAGUE OF LOVE IN ACTION

O LEAGUE of Kindness, woven in all lands,
    You bring Love's tender mercies in your hands;
Above all flags you lift the conquering sign,
And hold invincible Love's battle line.

O League of Kindness, in your far-flung bands,
You weave a chain that reaches to God's hands;
And where blind guns are plotting for the grave,
Yours are the lips that cheer, the arms that save.

O League of Kindness, in your flag we see
A foregleam of the brotherhood to be
In ages when the agonies are done,
When all will love and all will lift as one.
                                    EDWIN MARKHAM

MOTHER'S DAY

MOTHER

I HAVE praised many loved ones in my song,
          And yet I stand
Before her shrine, to whom all things belong,
          With empty hand.

Perhaps the ripening future holds a time
          For things unsaid;
Not now; men do not celebrate in rime
          Their daily bread.
                                    THERESA HELBURN

MY MOTHER

WHO ran to help me when I fell,
     And would some pretty story tell
Or kiss the place to make it well?
     My Mother.

JANE TAYLOR

YOU MEAN MY MOTHER

IF I were asked to give a thought which in one word
     would speak
A unity of brotherhood, a sympathy complete,
A hundred happy cheery ways, a mind that knows its own,
Contented midst a throng of folk, yet peaceful when alone,
A heart that sheds its silent glow, to brighten many an-
     other,
Without a moment of delay, I'd say, "You mean my
     mother."

UNKNOWN

NOBODY KNOWS—BUT MOTHER

NOBODY knows of the work it makes
     To keep the home together,
Nobody knows of the steps it takes,
     Nobody knows—but mother.

Nobody listens to childish woes,
     Which kisses only smother;
Nobody's pained by naughty blows,
     Nobody—only mother.

Nobody knows of the sleepless care
     Bestowed on baby brother;
Nobody knows of the tender prayer,
     Nobody—only mother.

Nobody knows of the lessons taught
   Of loving one another;
Nobody knows of the patience sought,
   Nobody—only mother.

Nobody knows of the anxious fears,
   Lest darlings may not weather
The storm of life in after years,
   Nobody knows—but mother.

Nobody kneels at the throne above
   To thank the Heavenly Father
For that sweetest gift—a mother's love;
   Nobody can—but mother.

UNKNOWN

WHEN MOTHER'S SICK

MY mother's sick to-day, an' gee—
   It makes me feel so bad to see
How sick she looks. But still she'll grin
Each time that I come sneakin' in.
You never hear my mother kick
When she is tired and feelin' sick.
She always says, and tries to smile:
"I'll be all right, Son—after while."

An' when I sit beside her bed,
She'll hold my hand and pat my head,
An' smile at me so sweet that I
Am awful 'fraid I'm goin' to cry—
An' pretty soon, I hear her say:
"If I were you, I'd run an' play."
An' then I squeeze her hand some more,
An' sneak out easy through the door.

But, I don't want to play and run,
For I don't feel like havin' fun
When Mother's sick—and too, my Dad
Just acts so funny like, and sad—

An' golly, he is grouchy, too;
But I don't think he's mad, do you?
I think he feels the same as me,
For he likes Mother, too, you see.

But she told me this afternoon
That she'd be better pretty soon.
An' gee, but I do hope she will,
For I have surely had my fill
Of eatin' things that Daddy cooks—
An' I don't like their taste nor looks!
I tell you what, when Mother's sick,
We want her better mighty quick!

WILLIAM HERSCHELL

MEMORIAL DAY

MEMORIAL DAY *

IS it enough to think to-day
    Of all our brave, then put away
The thought until a year has sped?
Is this full honor for our dead?

Is it enough to sing a song
And deck a grave; and all year long
Forget the brave who died that we
Might keep our great land proud and free?

Full service needs a greater toll—
That we who live give heart and soul
To keep the land they died to save,
And be ourselves, in turn, the brave!

ANNETTE WYNNE

* Reprinted by permission from *For Days and Days: A Year-round Treasury of Verse for Children*, by Annette Wynne; copyright, 1919, by Frederick A. Stokes Company.

A KNOT OF BLUE AND GRAY

YOU ask me why, upon my breast,
 Unchanged from day to day,
Linked side by side in this broad band,
 I wear the blue and gray.
I had two brothers long ago—
 Two brothers, blithe and gay;
One wore a suit of Northern blue,
 And one a suit of Southern gray.
One heard the roll call of the South,
 And linked his fate with Lee;
The other bore the Stars and Stripes
 With Sherman to the sea.

Each fought for what he deemed was right,
 And fell with sword in hand;
One sleeps amid Virginia's hills,
 And one by Georgia's strand,
But the same sun shines on both their graves,
 'Mid valley and o'er hill,
And in the darkest of the hours
 My brothers do live still.
And this is why, upon my breast,
 Unchanged from day to day,
Linked side by side in this broad band,
 I wear a knot of blue and gray.

UNKNOWN

REMEMBERING DAY

ALL the soldiers marching along;
 All the children singing a song;
All the flowers dewy and sweet;
All the flags hung out in the street;
Hearts that throb in a grateful way—
For this is our Remembering Day.

MARY WIGHT SAUNDERS

AMERICAN INDEPENDENCE

HAIL to the planting of Liberty's tree!
Hail to the charter declaring us free!
Millions of voices are chanting its praises,
Millions of worshipers bend at its shrine,
Wherever the sun of America blazes
Wherever the stars of our bright banner shine.

Sing to the heroes who breasted the flood
That, swelling, rolled o'er them—a deluge of blood,
Fearless they clung to the ark of the nation,
And dashed on 'mid lightning, and thunder, and blast,
Till Peace, like the dove, brought her breach of salvation,
And Liberty's mount was their refuge at last.

Bright is the beautiful land of our birth,
The home of the homeless all over the earth.
Oh! let us ever with fondest devotion,
The freedom our fathers bequeathed us, watch o'er
Till the angel shall stand on the earth and the ocean,
And shout 'mid earth's ruins, that Time is no more.

A. B. STREET

MEMORIAL DAY

WE plant the trees on Memorial Day,
For the soldiers who died long ago.
We plant them in the month of May
While cool winds still do blow.

ROSE FLORENCE LEVY

LET WAR'S TEMPESTS CEASE

LORD, let war's tempests cease,
Fold the whole world in peace
Under Thy wings.
Make all the nations one,

All hearts beneath the sun,
Till Thou shalt reign alone,
    Great Kings of Kings.
            HENRY WADSWORTH LONGFELLOW

FLAG DAY

THE FLAG GOES BY

HATS off!
    Along the street there comes
A blare of bugles, a ruffle of drums,
A flash of color beneath the sky:
Hats off!
The flag is passing by!

Blue and crimson and white it shines,
Over the steel-tipped, ordered lines.
Hats off!
The colors before us fly;
But more than the flag is passing by:

Sea fights and land fights, grim and great,
Fought to make and to save the State:
Weary marches and sinking ships;
Cheers of victory on dying lips;

Days of plenty and years of peace;
March of a strong land's swift increase;
Equal justice, and right and law,
Stately honor and reverend awe;

Sign of a nation, great and strong
To ward her people from foreign wrong:
Pride and glory and honor—all
Live in the colors to stand or fall.

Hats off!
Along the street there comes
A blare of bugles, a ruffle of drums;
And loyal hearts are beating high:
Hats off!
The flag is passing by!

HENRY HOLCOMB BENNETT

THE NEW PLEDGE TO THE FLAG

I PLEDGE allegiance to the Flag of the United States and to the Republic for which it stands, one nation, indivisible, with liberty and justice for all.

THE LITTLE FLAGS

OH, when you see them flying
  Beside the summer way—
The little flags they put in place
  Upon Memorial Day—
Remember each is crying
  A message straight to you—
A message straight to every lad
  Whose heart is clean and true.

They tell the splendid story
  Of those who marched away
In answer to a voice that said,
  "Your country calls! Obey!"
They heard the call to glory,
  As you can, if you try:
"Your flag demands your best to-day,
  Not some time, by and by!"

JOHN CLAIR MINOT

INDEPENDENCE DAY

FOURTH OF JULY ODE

OUR fathers fought for Liberty,
  They struggled long and well,
History of their deeds can tell—
But did they leave us free?

Are we free from vanity,
Free from pride, and free from self,
Free from love of power and pelf,
From everything that's beggarly?

Are we free from stubborn will,
From low hate and malice small,
From opinion's tyrant thrall?
Are none of us our own slaves still?

Are we free to speak our thought,
To be happy, and be poor,
Free to enter Heaven's door,
To live and labor as we ought?

Are we then made free at last
From the fear of what men say,
Free to reverence To-Day,
Free from the slavery of the Past?

Our fathers fought for liberty,
They struggled long and well,
History of their deeds can tell—
But ourselves must set us free.

JAMES RUSSELL LOWELL

Labor Day

TOIL

THERE'S a never dying chorus
    Breaking on the human ear;
In the busy town before us,
Voices loud, and deep, and clear.
This is labor's endless ditty;
This is toil's prophetic voice,
Sounding through the town and city,
Bidding human hearts rejoice.

Sweeter than the poet's singing
Is that anthem of the free;
Blither is the anvil's ringing
Than the song of bird or bee.
There's a glory in the rattle
Of the wheels 'mid factory gloom;
Richer than e'er snatched from battle
Or the trophies of the loom.

See the skillful mason raising
Gracefully yon towering pile;
Round the forge and furnace blazing,
Stand the noble men of toil.
They are heroes of the people,
Who the wealth of nations raise;
Every dome, and spire, and steeple
Raise their heads in labor's praise.

Glorious men of truth and labor,
Shepherds of the human fold,
That shall lay the brand and saber
With the barbarous things of old.
Priests and prophets of creation,
Bloodless heroes in the fight,
Toilers for the world's salvation,
Messengers of peace and light.

Speed the plow and speed the harrow;
Peace and plenty send abroad;
Better far the spade and barrow
Than the cannon or the sword.
Each invention, each improvement,
Renders weak oppression's rod;
Every sign and every movement
Brings us nearer truth and God.

UNKNOWN

COLUMBUS DAY

THE BOY COLUMBUS

" 'TIS a wonderful story," I hear you say,
    "How he struggled and worked and plead and
        prayed,
And faced every danger undismayed,
With a will that would neither break nor bend,
And discovered a new world in the end—
But what does it teach to a boy of to-day?
All the worlds are discovered, you know of course,
All the rivers are traced to their utmost source:
There is nothing left for a boy to find,
If he had ever so much a mind
    To become a discoverer famous;
And if we'd much rather read a book
About some one else, and the risks he took,
    Why nobody, surely, can blame us."

So you think all the worlds are discovered now;
All the lands have been charted and sailed about,
Their mountains climbed, their secrets found out;
All the seas have been sailed, and their currents known—
To the utmost isles the winds have blown
They have carried a venturing prow?
Yet there lie all about us new worlds, everywhere,
That await their discoverer's footfall; spread fair
Are electrical worlds that no eye has yet seen,

And mechanical worlds that lie hidden serene
   And await their Columbus securely.
There are new worlds in Science and new worlds in Art,
And the boy who will work with his head and his heart
   Will discover his new world surely.

UNKNOWN

COLUMBUS

LONG lay the ocean paths from man concealed;
   Light came from heaven—the magnet was revealed,
A surer star to guide the seaman's eye
Than the pale glory of the northern sky;
Alike ordained to shine by night and day,
Through calm and tempest, with unsettling ray;
Where'er the mountains rise, the billows roll,
Still with strong impulse turning to the pole,
True as the sun is to the morning true,
Though light as film, and trembling as the dew.

JAMES MONTGOMERY

ROOSEVELT DAY

THE ROOSEVELT CREED

I BELIEVE in honesty, sincerity, and the square deal; in making up one's mind what to do—and doing it.

I believe in fearing God and taking one's own part.

I believe in hitting the line hard when you are right.

I believe in hard work and honest sport.

I believe in a sane mind in a sane body.

I believe we have room for but one soul loyalty, and that is loyalty to the American people.

Christmas and New Year's

CAROL

WHEN the herds were watching
   In the midnight chill,
Came a spotless lambkin
   From the heavenly hill.

Snow was on the mountains,
   And the wind was cold,
When from God's own garden
   Dropped a rose of gold.

When 'twas bitter winter,
   Houseless and forlorn
In a star-lit stable
   Christ the Babe was born.

Welcome, heavenly lambkin;
   Welcome, golden rose;
Alleluia, Baby,
   In the swaddling clothes!

WILLIAM CANTON

CHRISTMAS IN THE HEART

IT is Christmas in the mansion,
   Yule-log fires and silken frocks;
It is Christmas in the cottage,
   Mother's filling little socks.

It is Christmas on the highway,
   In the thronging, busy mart;
But the dearest, truest Christmas
   Is the Christmas in the heart.

UNKNOWN

LONG, LONG AGO

WINDS through the olive trees
        Softly did blow,
Round little Bethlehem
    Long, long ago.

Sheep on the hillside lay
    Whiter than snow,
Shepherds were watching them,
    Long, long ago.

Then from the happy sky,
    Angels bent low
Singing their songs of joy,
    Long, long ago.

For in a manger bed,
    Cradled we know,
Christ came to Bethlehem,
    Long, long ago.

UNKNOWN

A CATCH BY THE HEARTH

SING we all merrily
    Christmas is here,
The day that we love best
    Of days in the year.

Bring forth the holly,
    The box, and the bay,
Deck out our cottage
    For glad Christmas Day.

Sing we all merrily,
    Draw around the fire,
Sister and brother,
    Grandson and sire.

UNKNOWN

A CHRISTMAS CAROL

WHEN Christ was born in Bethlehem,
         'Twas night but seemed the noon of day:
         The star whose light
         Was pure and bright,
Shone with unwav'ring ray;
         But one bright star,
         One glorious star
Guided the Eastern Magi from afar.

Then peace was spread throughout the land;
The lion fed beside the lamb;
         And with the kid,
         To pasture led,
The spotted leopard fed
         In peace, in peace
         The calf and bear,
The wolf and lamb reposed together there.

As shepherds watched their flocks by night,
An angel brighter than the sun
         Appeared in air,
         And gently said,
"Fear not, be not afraid,
         Behold, behold,
         Beneath your eye,
Earth has become a smiling Paradise."

TRANSLATED FROM THE NEAPOLITAN

A CHRISTMAS FOLK SONG

THE little Jesus came to town;
         The wind blew up, the wind blew down;
Out in the street the wind was bold;
Now who could house Him from the cold?

Then opened wide a stable door,
Fair were the rushes on the floor;
The Ox put forth a hornèd head:
"Come, little Lord, here make Thy bed."

Uprose the Sheep were folded near:
"Thou Lamb of God, come, enter here."
He entered there to rush and reed,
Who was the Lamb of God indeed.

The little Jesus came to town;
With ox and sheep He laid Him down;
Peace to the byre, peace to the fold,
For that they housed Him from the cold!

LIZETTE WOODWORTH REESE

KRISS KRINGLE

JUST as the moon was fading amid her misty rings,
And every stocking was stuffed with childhood's precious things,
Old Kriss Kringle looked around, and saw on the elm-tree bough,
High-hung, an oriole's nest, silent and empty now.

"Quite like a stocking," he laughed, "pinned up there on the tree!
Little I thought the birds expected a present from me!"
Then old Kriss Kringle, who loves a joke as well as the best,
Dropped a handful of flakes in the oriole's empty nest.

THOMAS BAILEY ALDRICH

A LETTER TO SANTA

DEAR Santa Claus:
                    Please bring to me,
A little tiny Christmas Tree.
I've never had one yet, you see—

And I just thought if I
Would write a note to you, and say:
"Please don't forget me Christmas Day"
You wouldn't pass me by.

I wrote you last year—don't you know?—
But maybe you were busy though
Or else your reindeers wouldn't go—
I don't know what it was.
But anyhow, you never came—
And I am *sure* I signed my name—
I'm Jimmy, Santa Claus!

I'm Jimmy Moore—have you forgot?
I think you have—you've never brought
One thing to me—but I just thought
If, once more, I would write,
A note, and ask you please to bring
Not very much—just anything—
Well—I just thought you might.

I'd like some toys, but I suppose
I'd better ask, instead, for clothes.
And, Santa Claus, my little toes
Stick right out in the air.
And gee-ma-nee! On days like these,
I tell you what, I nearly freeze!
But no one seems to care.

I guess that's all I'd better say—
But, won't you, please, come past our way,
And give me one real Christmas Day?
Forget that we are poor!
Our house is where it always was;
Try hard to find it, Santa Claus!
That's all. From
                                    Jimmy Moore.
                                    UNKNOWN

RING, JOYFUL BELLS!

RING, bells, from every lofty height!
　　An infant fair is born to-night;
Ring far and wide, ring full and clear,
To welcome in the glad New Year.
"The king is dead: long live the king!"
They said of old, and so we sing.
The Old Year has gone to his repose;
There let him rest beneath the snows.

Behind us, with the year that's gone,
Lie countless sins that we have done.
With joy we cast all care away,
And pass into another day.
New day, new life, whose noble deed
Will all our sinful years succeed.
A life of action, great and strong,
To cancel all we've done of wrong.

Ring, joyful bells! Our hearts beat high
With faith and hope, beyond the sky
Perchance the angels stand and wait
To catch the sound at heaven's gate.
And, echoing each silver tone,
Sing songs of praise around the throne.
Ring, happy bells! To us is given
Still longer to prepare for heaven.

VIOLET FULLER

EASTER

AT EASTER TIME

THE little flowers came through the ground,
　　At Easter time, at Easter time;
They raised their heads and looked around,
　　At happy Easter time.
And every pretty bud did say,

"Good people, bless this holy day,
For Christ is risen, the angels say
    At happy Easter time!"

The pure white lily raised its cup
    At Easter time, at Easter time;
The crocus to the sky looked up
    At happy Easter time.
"We'll hear the song of Heaven!" they say,
    "Its glory shines on us to-day.
Oh! may it shine on us always
    At holy Easter time!"

'Twas long and long and long ago,
    That Easter time, that Easter time;
But still the pure white lilies blow
    At happy Easter time.
And still each little flower doth say,
    "Good Christians, bless this holy day,
For Christ is risen, the angels say
    At blessed Easter time!"

LAURA E. RICHARDS

APRIL AND MAY

APRIL cold with dropping rain
    Willows and lilacs brings again,
The whistle of returning birds,
And the trumpet-lowing of the herds.
The scarlet maple-keys betray
What potent blood hath modest May,
What fiery force the earth renews,
The wealth of forms, the flush of hues;
What joy in rosy waves outpoured
Flows from the heart of Love, the Lord.

RALPH WALDO EMERSON

NATURE'S CREED

I BELIEVE in the brook as it wanders
  From hillside into glade;
I believe in the breeze as it whispers
  When evening's shadows fade.
I believe in the roar of the river
  As it dashes from high cascade;
I believe in the cry of the tempest
  'Mid the thunder's cannonade.
I believe in the light of shining stars,
  I believe in the sun and the moon;
I believe in the flash of lightning,
  I believe in the night bird's croon.
I believe in the faith of the flowers,
  I believe in the rock and sod,
For in all of these appeareth clear
  The handiwork of God.

UNKNOWN

EASTER

I GOT me flowers to strew Thy way,
  I got me boughs off many a tree.
But Thou wast up at break of day
And broughtst Thy sweets along with Thee.

The Sun arising in the East,
Though he give light and th' East perfume,
If they should offer to contest
With Thy arising, they presume.

Can there be any day but this,
Though many suns to shine endeavor?
We count three hundred but we miss:
There is but one, and that one ever.

GEORGE HERBERT

Thanksgiving

THE FEAST TIME OF THE YEAR

THIS is the feast time of the year,
　　When plenty pours her wine of cheer,
'And even humble boards may spare
To poorer poor a kindly share.
While bursting barns and granaries know
A richer, fuller overflow,
And they who dwell in golden ease
Bless without toil, yet toil to please.
This is the feast time of the year,
The blessed advent draweth near;
Let rich and poor together break
The bread of love for Christ's sweet sake,
Against the time when rich and poor
Must ope for Him a common door,
Who comes a guest, yet makes a feast,
And bids the greatest and the least.

UNKNOWN

THANKSGIVING DAY *

BRAVE and high-souled Pilgrims, you who knew no
　　fears,
How many words to thankfulness go ringing down the
years;
May we follow after; like you, work and pray,
And with hearts of thankfulness keep Thanksgiving Day.

ANNETTE WYNNE

* Reprinted by permission from *For Days and Days: A Year-round Treasury of Verse for Children*, by Annette Wynne; copyright, 1919, by Frederick A. Stokes Company.

PRAISE GOD

PRAISE God for wheat, so white and sweet,
Of which to make our bread!
Praise God for yellow corn, with which
His waiting world is fed!
Praise God for fish and flesh and fowl
He gave to men for food!
Praise God for every creature which
He made and called it good!

Praise God for winter's store of ice,
Praise God for summer's heat!
Praise God for fruit trees bearing seed,
"To you it is for meat!"
Praise God for all the bounty
By which the world is fed!
Praise God, ye children all, to whom
He gives your daily bread!

UNKNOWN

THANKSGIVING

FOR raiment and for daily bread,
For shelter from the rain and shine,
For length of days and hardihead,
Small gratitude is mine.

These are the laborer's due hire,
Though hard it be to solve the doubt
How I have merited the fire
My brother goes without.

But for the mission of my feet,
The labor of my heart and hand,
The service, difficult and sweet
And all my own, I stand

Most deeply thankful, and for art
  That nerves my strength and fires my brain,
For song, that ever calls my heart
  Back to its dreams again.

For the assurance that my toil
  Is furthering some mighty end
Beyond the present strife and moil,
  Toward which the ages trend;

For labor, wageless though it be,
  For what I give, not what I take,
For battle, not for victory,
  My prayer of thanks I make.

ODELL SHEPARD

SINGING THE REAPERS HOMEWARD COME

SINGING the reapers homeward come, Io! Io!
  Merrily singing the harvest home, Io! Io!
  Along the field, along the road,
Where autumn is scattering leaves abroad,
Homeward cometh the ripe last load, Io! Io!

Singers are filling the twilight dim
With cheerful song, Io! Io!
The spirit of song ascends to Him
  Who causeth the corn to grow.
He freely sent the gentle rain,
The summer sun glorified hill and plain,
To golden perfection brought the grain, Io! Io!

Silently, nightly, fell the dew,
Gently the rain, Io! Io!
But who can tell how the green corn grew,
  Or who beheld it grow?
Oh! God, the good, in sun and rain,
He'd look'd on the flourishing fields of grain,
Till they all appear'd on hill and plain
  Like living gold, Io Io!

UNKNOWN

MANNERS

GOLDEN KEYS

A BUNCH of golden keys is mine,
   To make each day with gladness shine.
"Good Morning," that's the golden key
That unlocks every day for me.
When evening comes, "Good Night," I say,
And close the door of each glad day.
When at the table, "If you please,"
I take from off my bunch of keys.
When friends give anything to me,
I'll use the little "Thank You" key.
"Excuse Me," "Beg Your Pardon," too,
When by mistake some harm I do;
Or, if unkindly harm I've given,
With "Forgive Me" I shall be forgiven.
On a golden ring these keys I'll bind;
This is its motto, "Be Ye Kind."
I'll often use each golden key,
And then a child polite I'll be.

UNKNOWN

IF I WERE YOU

WHAT would I do if I were you?
   First thing, I'd make a rule
To put my hat and boots in place
   When I came home from school.

What would I do if I were you?
   I wouldn't pout and cry
Because I couldn't have my way
   About a piece of pie.
179

What would I do if I were you?
  I'd speak a pleasant word
To this and that one in the house
  And not be sour as curd.

What would I do if I were you?
  I'd not fly off apace
Into a raging passion when
  Another took my place.

And when a body asked my help,
  I'd try to do a favor,
So that it should not always have
  A disobliging flavor.

If I were you, my little friend,
  I'd try to be so good,
That my example, all around
  Might follow if they could.

Then 'twill be easy to obey
  His law and parents' rule;
And you'll be happy, too, and good,
  At home, or play, or school.

UNKNOWN

POLITENESS

GOOD little boys should never say
    "I will," and "Give me these";
O, no! that never is the way,
  But "Mother, if you please."

And "If you please," to Sister Ann
  Good boys to say are ready;
And, "Yes, sir," to a Gentleman,
  And, "Yes, ma'am," to a Lady.

ELIZABETH TURNER

PRIMER LESSON *

LOOK out how you use proud words.
  When you let proud words go, it is not easy to call
    them back.
They wear long boots, hard boots; they walk off proud;
    they can't hear you calling—
Look out how you use proud words.

CARL SANDBURG

ANGER

ANGER is a bad, bad man,
  He will catch me if he can,
And lock me in a tower high
  Reaching up into the sky.

Far away from Mother dear,
  Way up high where none can hear;
But if I a good child be,
  Mother says he can't get me!

LILLY ROBINSON

* From *Slabs of the Sunburnt West* by Carl Sandburg; copyright,
1922, by Harcourt, Brace and Company, Inc.

SCHOOL DAYS

SALUTATORY

MY teacher said that I must speak
A piece to welcome you,
And so her word I will obey,
As boys should always do.

I hope, of course, it may be "well"
That you have "come" to-day
To see us all dressed in our best
And hear what we will say.

Indeed we'd like it if you'd come
Our lessons all to hear,
And not just on this closing day,
Which comes but once a year.

There is a great big word they use
I'll try to tell it straight,
It's co-co, I have it now,
It's just coöperate.

It means that you must help us all
In what we say and do.
Teachers and boys and girls, each one—
'Twill be such fun for you.

And so when next year rolls around
Do please remember this,
If you must wait till closing day
A lot of fun you'll miss.

It's well for us that you have come
To keep this festive day;
When big folks notice little folks
It helps them on their way.

And if you'll take the time to come
  When we our lessons say
We'll welcome you as heartily
  As I do now to-day.

CLARA J. DENTON

THE BEST DAY

IF I could choose the best day
  In all the long, long year,
I would choose just this one,
  Which we have right here.

O, yes, this is the best day,
  The best for you and me,
Shuts the schoolroom door tight,
  Setting us all free.

Good-by to foggy lessons,
  The summer's on the way,
Now we're out for frolics,
  For 'tis our closing day.

CLARA J. DENTON

AFTER VACATION THOUGHTS

I WISHT I was a little rock
  A'settin' on a hill;
A'doin' nothing all day long
  But just a'settin' still.
I wouldn't eat, I wouldn't drink,
  I wouldn't even wash,
I'd set and set a thousand years
  And rest myself, by gosh.

R. O. C.

GRAMMAR IN A NUTSHELL

I

Three little words you often see
Are articles—a, an, and the.

II

A noun's the name of anything,
As school or garden, hoop or swing.

III

Adjectives, the kind of noun,
As great, small, pretty, white, or brown.

IV

Instead of nouns the pronouns stand—
Her head, his face; your arm, my hand.

V

Verbs tell something to be done—
To read, count, laugh, sing, jump, or run.

VI

How things are done the adverbs tell,
As slowly, quickly, ill, or well.

VII

Conjunctions join the words together,
As men and women, wind or weather.

VIII

The preposition stands before
A noun, as in or through the door.

IX

The interjection shows surprise,
As oh! how pretty! ah! how wise!

X

The whole are called nine parts of speech,
Which reading, writing, speaking teach.

UNKNOWN

THE BOY AND HIS TOP

A LITTLE Boy had bought a Top,
     The best in all the toyman's shop;
He made a whip with good eel's skin,
He lash'd the top, and made it spin;
All the children within call,
And the servants, one and all,
Stood round to see it and admire.
At last the Top began to tire,
He cried out, "Pray don't hit me, Master,
You whip too hard—I can't spin faster,
I can spin quite as well without it."
The little Boy replied, "I doubt it;
I only whip you for your good,
You were a foolish lump of wood,
By dint of whipping you were raised
To see yourself admired and praised,
And if I left you, you'd remain
A foolish lump of wood again."

EXPLANATION

Whipping sounds a little odd,
I don't mean whipping with a rod,
It means to teach a boy incessantly,
Whether by lessons or more pleasantly,
Every hour and every day,
By every means in every way,
By reading, writing, riming, talking,
By riding to see sights, and walking:
If you leave off he drops at once,
A lumpish, wooden-headed dunce.

JOHN HOOKHAM FRERE

A B C

OH, thou alphabetic row,
     Fun and freedom's early foe;
Shall I e'er forget the primer,

Or the teacher Mrs. Trimmer—
Or the problem then so vast,
Whether Z was first or last?
All Pandora had for me
Was emptied forth in A B C.

Curious letters—single—double,
Source of many a childish trouble,
How I strove with pouting pain
To get thee quarter'd on my brain.
But when the giant feat was done,
How noble was the field I'd won!
Wit, wisdom, reason, rime—the key
To all their wealth but A B C.

Ye really ought to be exempt
From slighting taunt and cool contempt
But, drinking deep from learning's cup
We scorn the hand that filled it up.
Be courteous, pedants—stay and thank
Your servants of the Roman rank,
For F. R. S. and LL.D.
Can only follow A B C.

ELIZA COOK

INDEX OF AUTHORS

A

B

U

V

W

INDEX OF TITLES

A

B

C

INDEX OF FIRST LINES

A

B

C

D

Y

BOOKS FOR YOUNGER READERS

THE JOY STREET BOOKS
Supremely beautiful books for children by groups of famous writers and illustrators. Each year a "Joy Street" book appears, filled with stories and poems of gay humor and happy fancy. Illustrated in color and black and white. Each, $2.50.

ALICE IN JUNGLELAND
By Mary Hastings Bradley. The famous novelist tells most delightfully of her little daughter's adventures in African wilds. Illustrated by Alice. $2.00.

THROUGH THE LANE OF STARS
By Sister M. Eleanore. The life-stories of famous saints, beautifully told for young people. Illustrated. $2.00.

ADVENTURES OF TOM MARVEL
Ralph Henry Barbour in an exciting tale of three youthful runaways. Illustrated. $1.50.

THE JANITOR'S CAT
Theodore Acland Harper's quaint story of a book-store cat who comes out at night to meet Dr. Doolittle, Alice, Peter Pan, the Grand Buffalo and other famous story-book characters. Illustrated. $2.00.

THE UNCLE WIGGILY BOOK
By Howard R. Garis. The familiar rabbit man, Baby Bunty and others in a wonderful group of stories. Illustrated in two colors. $1.75.

CHILDREN OF MANY LANDS
James Fairgrieve and Ernest Young take their readers on a visit to the children of other countries. Illustrated. $1.25.

HOMES FAR AWAY
By James Fairgrieve and Ernest Young. The home life of Eskimos, Lapps, Australians, Zulus and other peoples in a splendid account. Illustrated. $1.25.

RECITATIONS FOR YOUNGER CHILDREN
Grace Gaige edits this charming collection of readings. Something for almost every occasion and every time of year. $2.00.

D. APPLETON AND COMPANY
PUBLISHERS   NEW YORK